LIGON DUNCAN

1 & 2 THESSALONIANS FOR YOU

1 & 2 Thessalonians For You

© Ligon Duncan, 2023

Published by:
The Good Book Company

thegoodbook.com | thegoodbook.co.uk
thegoodbook.com.au | thegoodbook.co.nz | thegoodbook.co.in

Published in association with the literary agency of Wolgemuth & Associates.

ISBN: 9781784985011 | JOB-007279 | Printed in India

Cover design by Ben Woodcraft

CONTENTS

SERIES PREFACE

Each volume of the *God's Word For You* series takes you to the heart of a book of the Bible, and applies its truths to your heart.

The central aim of each title is to be:

- Bible centered
- Christ glorifying
- Relevantly applied
- Easily readable

You can use *1 & 2 Thessalonians For You:*

To read. You can simply read from cover to cover, as a book that explains and explores the themes, encouragements and challenges of this part of Scripture.

To feed. You can work through this book as part of your own personal regular devotions, or use it alongside a sermon or Bible-study series at your church. Each chapter is divided into two (or occasionally three) shorter sections, with questions for reflection at the end of each.

To lead. You can use this as a resource to help you teach God's word to others, both in small-group and whole-church settings. You'll find tricky verses or concepts explained using ordinary language, and helpful themes and illustrations along with suggested applications.

These books are not commentaries. They assume no understanding of the original Bible languages, nor a high level of biblical knowledge. Verse references are marked in **bold** so that you can refer to them easily. Any words that are used rarely or differently in everyday language outside the church are marked in gray when they first appear, and are explained in a glossary toward the back. There, you'll also find details of resources you can use alongside this one, in both personal and church life.

Our prayer is that as you read, you'll be struck not by the contents of this book, but by the book it's helping you open up; and that you'll praise not the author of this book, but the One he is pointing you to.

Carl Laferton, Series Editor

Bible translations used:

ESV: English Standard Version (this is the version being quoted unless otherwise stated)

NIV: New International Version

INTRODUCTION TO THESSALONIANS

Have you ever had a conversation with someone in which they said, "You know, Christianity is all about escape. It's all about 'pie in the sky by and by'. You Christians think that what's here doesn't really matter"? I've read this kind of charge more in recent times than I used to 20 or 30 years ago. The theory goes that until we Christians jettison our escapism—our thinking about the future, the promises of heaven, the return of Christ—we're really not going to be able to do a good job of living *this* life. If our faith is all about heaven, we Christians will fail to invest ourselves in this world, to care for the needy and for the poor, and to serve in such a way as to truly help our fellow humans. Until we give up our 'pie in the sky by and by,' the charge goes, we're never really going to be any earthly good.

That charge misses the entire point of all of the teaching in the Bible about the end of this world and the return of Jesus. Scripture is written not so that we do not care about this life but to enable us to live this life well. That's what we find in 1 and 2 Thessalonians. The writer, **Paul**, spends a lot of time in these two letters talking about the future—and in every chapter, we also see him showing how this future relates to our daily lives now. Paul's point is that our eternal confidence does not rob us of the capacity to care; it empowers us to care. In fact, you cannot live this life well if you're not living it in light of the resurrection and of the second coming of Christ.

Paul's first letter to the Thessalonian church is one of the very earliest parts of the New Testament (it is probably Paul's first letter, though that may have been Galatians), with his second letter following a matter of months later. They were written less than 20 years after Jesus died and rose again. And they are filled with references to the second coming of Jesus Christ. That should not surprise us. After all, faith in Jesus doesn't make sense without the resurrection of Jesus and his future return. In fact, without those things, Paul says that he and his fellow Christians would be "of all people most to be pitied" (1 Corinthians 15:19). And so, here, Paul is telling some of his earliest readers how important it is for them to hope in the return of Jesus.

The letters were written to a young church plant, set up by Paul during his missionary trip to the Roman province of Macedonia (in modern-day Greece) in AD 49 or 50. Thessalonica was the capital of and largest city in Macedonia, and was a busy seaport numbering around 200,000 inhabitants. Acts 17:1-10 tells us the story of how Paul preached in the **synagogue** there, "explaining and proving that it was necessary for the Christ to suffer and to rise from the dead, and saying, 'This Jesus, whom I proclaim to you, is the Christ'" (Acts 17:3). As is the pattern in Acts, some believed, and many did not. Before long, Paul and his companions were forced out of the city as a result of a riot stirred up by some of those synagogue members who had rejected the gospel. Paul's time with this fledgling church was therefore short; and, having passed through Berea and Athens and on to Corinth, he awaited news of these new believers with some anxiety (1 Thessalonians 3:5). So when Timothy returned to Thessalonica and then came to Paul in Corinth to report that the Thessalonian church was holding firm to the faith and remaining loyal to the gospel he had taught them, despite facing persecution from its inception, Paul was overjoyed:

"In all our distress and affliction we have been comforted about you through your faith. For now we live, if you are standing fast in the Lord. For what thanksgiving can we return to God for you, for all the joy that we feel for your sake before our God." (1 Thessalonians 3:7-9)

Paul's love for the churches he had founded by God's **grace** is on full display in his first letter to the Thessalonians as he explains his abrupt departure (1 Thessalonians 2) and encourages these Christians to live to please God—that is, to grow in godliness—in their relationships, their work, their mourning, and their honoring of their leaders (chapters 3 – 5). His second letter, presumably sent in response to the news he had received from those who took his first to Thessalonica, implies that the persecution had worsened and had become unremitting; Paul felt the need to explain why Christians face such suffering and how to continue in faith and love in the face of it. Again, his exhortation is centered on the coming return of the Lord Jesus, along with an assurance that that day has not already occurred, and on how to endure such trials and live life in light of Jesus' certain future coming.

So, as John Stott describes, these letters open a window onto a newly planted church in the middle of the 1st century—telling us "how it came into being, what the apostle taught it, what were its strengths and weaknesses, its theological and moral problems, and how it was spreading the gospel" (*The Message of Thessalonians*, p 20). It is striking how these two letters speak to our churches in the 21st century too. We, too, need to heed the call to remember that we are waiting for Jesus, the risen Son of God, to return from heaven. We, too, need to remember that church leadership and church membership are first and foremost about love—love for God and love for his people, in deed as well as in word. We, too, need to be exhorted to live to please God in our lives, whether in the home or at work. We, too, need the gospel to shape us such that Paul could say of our fellowships what he said of this young, persecuted Thessalonian church:

"You became imitators of us and of the Lord, for you received the word ... with the joy of the Holy Spirit, so that you became an example to all the believers ... Not only has the word of the Lord sounded forth from you ... but your faith in God has gone forth everywhere." (1 Thessalonians 1:6-8)

Ligon Duncan and Carl Laferton (Series Editor)

1. LIFE-DEFINING

The first four verses of this letter contain a greeting (**1:1***), a summary of a prayer (**v 2-3**), and a truth (**v 4**). In his greeting, Paul explains in a brief set of words who the Thessalonian believers really are—and it's a life-defining salutation. In his prayers, he thanks God for the way God has transformed their lives. And then in the truth, he lays out how they got here: how they went from being **polytheistic pagans** to being living, breathing believers in the one true God.

A Life-Defining Greeting

In **verse 1**, after greeting them in his own name and in the name of his partners, Paul addresses his recipients: "To the church of the Thessalonians." That's not too surprising—this is the gathering of believers in the town of **Thessalonica†**. But then he says something key: "in God the Father and the Lord Jesus Christ." This is a life-defining greeting that tells them who they are.

I normally don't pay much attention to the greetings in letters I receive, but there are some letters that repay such attention. For instance, the start of a love letter oftentimes contains a greeting that tells the reader where they stand. If I received a letter starting with "To the love of my life"—well, it would have my full attention! And Paul begins here in a way that deserves our full attention too: *You're in Thessalonica,* he says, *and you are also in God the Father and the Lord Jesus Christ. You are united to God by the Spirit in Jesus Christ. You are in him. You're under his protection. You're close to his heart.*

---

* All 1 & 2 Thessalonians verse references being looked at in each chapter part are in **bold**.
† Words in **gray** are defined in the Glossary (page 209).

You're underneath his gaze. You're the apple of his eye. You're in him. You're connected to him. You're with him. You're his. That's who you are, believers.

One of my now-retired colleagues at the seminary I serve, in Jackson, Mississippi, Dale Ralph Davis, used to sign his notes, "In Christ in Jackson, Dale." That was how he conceived of himself. He was in Christ, and he was in Jackson. He was in Jackson geographically, and he was in Christ spiritually. Paul wants the Thessalonians in the very first verse of his letter to them to remember that what defines them is not what street they grew up on, not who their parents are, not what groups they were a part of in high school and college, nor what they spend their time doing now—it's that they are "in God the Father and in the Lord Jesus Christ."

Then, still as part of his greeting, Paul gives a blessing. "Grace to you and peace"—these are glorious, big words. Grace is not just unmerited favor, nor is it just favor from God; it is special favor from God—saving favor from him that we did not earn or deserve. In fact, it is a saving favor that we demerited. We positively did not deserve for that favor to be shown to us. We rebelled against God. We did not believe in his word. In our pride, we rose up against him and worshiped idols, loving, trusting, and serving other things as our **functional** gods. We followed our own wills and walked in our own ways—and yet, in his love and mercy and grace, he saved us. This grace is what defines a Christian. Fundamentally, the Thessalonian Christians are recipients of grace.

They're also recipients of the peace that comes from that grace. This is not just about a cessation of hostility but total well-being. God's grace has as its design that you would experience total well-being as you worship him.

This is who the Thessalonian church is: believers in Christ, full of grace and peace. This is who we are as believers today too. It should hit us every once in a while. This is us! This greeting is life-defining. It shows us, as it showed the Thessalonians, who we really are.

Prayers of Thanksgiving

Next Paul describes how he prays in thanksgiving to God (**v 2-3**). These verses reveal an expression of gratitude to God for the grace-transformed lives of the Thessalonians. "We give thanks to God always for all of you, constantly mentioning you in our prayers." **Verse 3** tells us what he is thanking God *for*: "your work of faith and labor of love and steadfastness of hope in our Lord Jesus Christ."

Don't miss the significance of the phrase that comes before that, though: Paul remembers these things "before our God and Father." *Our*. This Jewish **apostle** is reminding the residents of this Greek city that their Christian life is a life together: it is about "our"—not "my"—"God and Father." Paul was a Jewish **Pharisee** and persecutor of Jewish Christians; but now he is the apostle to the **Gentiles**. Greeks and Jews may have been historically divided, and they may have been culturally very different, but now, in Christ, they were on the same team and in the same family. God is *our* Father.

How can Paul be so confident that the recipients of his letter are fellow believers with him? (After all, he was with them in Thessalonica for only a brief time.) Because he sees evidence of God's grace in their lives—and he sees it in three ways.

First, he knows about their "work of faith." Here's a truth that undermines the charge that Christianity makes us no earthly good. What does true faith result in? Work! Faith moves the believer to care—to care for others, to care for those in need, to care for those who are in times of trial and difficulty, and to care in sharing the gospel. Paul will come back to this in verses 6-10.

Second, Paul knows of their "labor of love." Labor means toil. It is hard work; it is obedience. And it results from the love of God, which is implanted in our hearts by the Spirit of God. Love moves us to toil in obedience, to toil for the gospel—not grudgingly, because we have to, but joyfully, because we get to. We are laboring for the Lord we love.

Third, Paul has noted their "steadfastness of hope." These folks hope in Jesus Christ. They hope in his resurrection and in his return, and that gives them endurance as they face (as we shall see) problems and persecutions. Resurrection hope is what keeps believers walking forwards when following **the Way** proves hard and broader roads look tempting.

Every church minister wants to see God's grace at work in the hearts of people. And here the apostle Paul is effectively saying to this church, which by God's grace he was able to found, *I see the work of God's grace abundantly evident in you—in your faith and love and hope, and in the work and labor and steadfastness it issues into. It gives me such joy, and so I thank God because that's him at work in you!*

The Truth of God's Electing Love

In **verse 4**, Paul moves on to teaching his readers a truth. The question is: how did these Thessalonians go from being pagan idolaters to being people whose lives were transformed by grace and who so clearly evidenced faith and love and hope? The answer is this: "For we know, brothers loved by God, that he has chosen you…" Paul knows that the Thessalonians are elect—chosen by God. He knows this not through some apostolic **word of knowledge** but because he sees their faith and love and hope. Faith that works, love that labors, and hope that stands firm: these are marks of those whom God has chosen.

This language of "elect" or "chosen" is language which was first used of Israel in the Old Testament. Out of all the nations, God chose Israel to be his own people. They were to bear witness to his name. Further to that, in the Old Testament we see some individuals who are spoken of as being chosen by God. Aaron was specially chosen by God as high priest (Numbers 17:1-8). No one could be a priest in the Old Testament who was not of Aaron's tribe because God had chosen Aaron. Then there were the kings of Israel—Saul and then David and his descendants. These were the kings chosen to rule over God's people. God specially set his love on David and told him that he would never lack a descendant to sit on his throne (2 Samuel 7:11b-16). David's family had been chosen.

God chose a people, a priest, and a king. In the New Testament, all of that glorious language of God choosing is applied to believers in our Lord Jesus Christ—whether they are Jew or Greek, slave or free, male or female (Galatians 3:28). If you read this as a believer in the Lord Jesus, you are one of the chosen of God. What that means is that trillions of years ago—before there was an earth, before there was this solar system, before there was this expanse of space that is 13.8 billion light-years across, before there was time—God set his love on you. *He chose you.* Paul writes 1 Thessalonians **1:4** because he wants these 1st-century believers to take that in: "Brothers loved by God ... *he has chosen you*" (my emphasis). It's the same as what he does in Ephesians 1:4-5: "He chose us in him before the foundation of the world ... In love he **predestined** us for adoption to himself as sons."

Paul wants the Thessalonian Christians to understand that their salvation began with the love of God. It didn't begin with them being better

> Their salvation began with the love of God. Paul wants them to be awash in that reality.

than other people. It didn't begin with them being more deserving than other people. It didn't begin with them figuring out these spiritual realities so that they placed their faith in Christ. It began with the love of God, before the world began. Paul wants them to be awash in that reality. He wants us to marvel at it too.

There's an old hymn by Isaac Watts called, "How Sweet and Awesome Is the Place," which helps us do just that. Watts drew on Jesus' **parable** of the wedding banquet (Matthew 22:1-10). In the parable, there's a royal wedding feast for the heir to the throne, but the invited guests won't come. So the king sends out his servants to go and gather folks from the highways and byways to come in and sit down at the marriage feast. It's a picture of the ultimate marriage feast: the wedding banquet of the **Lamb**, the Son of God, to which you and I are invited.

Watts' hymn helps us to stand in awe of the truth Paul has stated in 1 Thessalonians **1:4**. He poses a question:

Why was I made to hear thy voice,
And enter while there's room,
When thousands make a wretched choice,
And rather starve than come?

And the answer?

'Twas the same love that spread the feast
That sweetly forced us in;
Else we had still refused to taste,
And perished in our sin.

Paul wants the Thessalonians to know this. This is why they're not pagan polytheists anymore. It's because trillions of years ago God set his love on them. He had been pursuing them before time, before they were even born.

The **doctrine** of election is one that many struggle with and even reject. But here, Paul is making it clear that our experience of the love of God is rooted in an understanding that his love is an electing love. It has to be, because only electing love is unconditional love. Only electing love relies on nothing that we are or do, since it was bestowed upon us from before the creation of the world. And therefore we cannot lose it through anything that we are or do (Romans 8:37-39). God's election of his people is both the outworking of and the guarantee of his love for them.

I know a lot of godly Christians who struggle to really believe that God loves them in this way. It may be that there is some sin in the past or in the present which has undermined your confidence and your assurance of his love. You just think, "There is no way that God could love me because of what I did." It may be that your experience of human relationships has deeply impacted your ability to feel and to receive love—to know that you are truly loved. Most of us struggle to grasp this kind of unconditional, unlimited, electing love. And so God gives much time and space in his Scripture to this issue of his people knowing how much he loves them. We need to hear it!

Specifically here Paul—and the Spirit, who was inspiring his every word in this letter—knew that the Thessalonians needed to hear it. Before Paul even gets out of his greeting and his opening prayer, he wants you and me to go back and realize how much the Father loves us: because when we just begin to understand this world-preceding love, it is life-defining.

Questions for reflection

1. Our identity is tied up lots of things—what we do, where we're from, what we look like—but we've seen that the most important thing is that we are "in Christ." Why is that so liberating? How will it affect your day-to-day to remember that this is your most fundamental identity?

2. Where do you see the work of God's grace in those around you? How could you encourage them with that? What about in your own life?

3. What makes you doubt God's love for you? How does it help to remember that God chose you before the world began?

PART TWO

1 Thessalonians **1:5-6** are a continuation of Paul's description of his thanks for the Thessalonian church that he began in verse 2. He's telling these believers the content of his prayers to encourage them about the reality of their faith. Before he calls them to live in light of Jesus' return, Paul pauses to thank God for things that he has seen God doing in their lives. He does this precisely to prepare them for the **exhortations** that he is going to give them later in the letter.

These two verses teach us two key truths. In **verse 5**, Paul draws attention to the fact that the gospel is powerful. It's not just words; it comes with power, and this verse shows us how. And then in **verse 6**, he talks about the evidences of God's grace in the Thessalonian believers, which is just as relevant for believers today: what the Holy Spirit does in someone as they receive the gospel.

The Gospel Comes in Power

"Our gospel came to you not only in word, but also in power and in the Holy Spirit and with full conviction" (**v 5**). Notice first that the gospel has to come in words. Sometimes people talk about sharing the gospel wordlessly. It can't be done. The gospel is by definition an announcement; it is an announcement about something that God has done. God, in his love, has given his only Son, the Lord Jesus Christ, to die in the place of sinners—his enemies. Jesus lived, died, and rose in order that, while we were yet in our sin and ungodliness, we might be forgiven, that the dominion of sin might be broken in our lives, and that we might be accepted back into God's family and dwell with him forever. That is the gospel.

Sometimes Christian leaders say things like, "Be the gospel." They mean that you should live in a way that reflects the gospel, and that will be enough to draw people to Christ. Of course, there is truth in that. We must practice what we preach. We will want to demonstrate the results and the effects of the gospel in our lives so that people understand that we're not hypocrites; we're not saying one thing but living another way. We will want to show them that we love them and, by that, prepare them to hear the word of God. (Paul will move on to this in verse 9.) Those are good things, but they are not the gospel as such. The work of Christ on the cross is the gospel. Our job is not to be the gospel but to share it. And for that, we need words.

Actually, we need more than words: we need God's power. Fortunately, by God's grace, the gospel comes "also in power and in the Holy Spirit and with full conviction" (**v 5**). Here, Paul is thanking God that when he preached the gospel in Thessalonica, it didn't just come in his words; it came with converting, saving power. The Holy Spirit was at work, and this resulted in "full conviction"—that is, an assurance of its truth—on the part of these believers.

Paul is pointing to the fact that the word of God is powerful, and active, and sharper than any two-edged sword (Hebrews 4:12). "The gospel ... is the power of God for salvation" (Romans 1:16). It is an announcement that came with power to the Thessalonians, so that the Thessalonians saw that the gospel is not just words. The gospel makes sense of this life, provides an answer to the fear of death, tells us about our place in the world, and cleanses us of guilt and sin. The word of God comes in power—changing perspectives and transforming lives. It did then, and it still does today.

The Power Is the Spirit

It's important, and glorious, that Paul adds, "and in the Holy Spirit" (1 Thessalonians **1:5**). "Our gospel came to you ... in the Holy Spirit." Here is why. When the Thessalonians heard the gospel preached, the Holy Spirit opened their eyes. That is how the gospel came "with power." God worked so that Paul's listeners were fully on board with what Paul was preaching.

In the last chapter of the Gospel of Luke, right before Jesus ascends into heaven, he says to his disciples, "I am sending the promise of my Father upon you" (Luke 24:49). What is the promise of his Father?

Luke's sequel, Acts, answers that question very quickly. It describes the same scene as that at the end of Luke 24: the conversation that Jesus had with his disciples before he ascended. Here, Jesus says, "You will receive power when the Holy Spirit has come upon you" (Acts 1:8). So putting these two thoughts together, we have "I am going to send the promise of my Father … You will receive power when the Holy Spirit comes upon you."

As we reach Acts 2, we find **Peter** preaching at **Pentecost** to a huge crowd. His audience believe his message, are cut to the heart, and cry out, "What shall we do?" (v 37). What does Peter say? "Repent and be baptized every one of you in the name of Jesus Christ for the forgiveness of your sins, and you will receive the gift of the Holy Spirit. For the promise is for you and for your children and for all who are far off, everyone whom the Lord our God calls to himself" (v 38-39).

Throughout the book of Acts, wherever the gospel goes, the Holy Spirit comes. Wherever the gospel is accepted, the Holy Spirit is at work. He comes to convert, and he comes to **sanctify**—that's how he manifests himself. Luke is showing us that Jesus' words are being fulfilled over and over and over again. "I am sending the promise of my Father," Jesus assured his disciples. What is that promise? It is the Holy Spirit.

In Galatians 3:14 Paul says that Christ came so that "the blessing of **Abraham** might come to the Gentiles, so that we might receive the promised Spirit through faith." Paul is putting three things together: the promise, the Spirit, and God's blessing to Abraham. The sending of the Spirit is the fulfillment of God's blessing to Abraham in the **covenant** of grace made all the way back in Genesis 12, 15, and 17! When the gospel comes and the Holy Spirit changes our hearts and we receive it, we become recipients—all of us, Jews and Gentiles— of the blessing that God promised to give to Abraham thousands of years ago.

This is what Paul saw happen when he preached the word of God to the Thessalonians. The Holy Spirit opened their eyes to see that the gospel was true. They believed, and they received the promise that God had made to Abraham thousands of years ago—the promised Holy Spirit.

Joy in Affliction: An Evidence of Grace

How was the Spirit manifested in Thessalonica? That is the subject of 1 Thessalonians **1:6**: "You became imitators of us and of the Lord." The new Christians in Thessalonica started to live their lives the way Paul and the other Christians lived, and to have the same priorities that they had, because they had come to believe the same things Paul and the others believed. But the big thing that Paul wants to draw attention to is this: "You received the word in much affliction, with the joy of the Holy Spirit." This was the thing Paul saw the Holy Spirit do most dramatically in them: in much affliction, they had joy. That joy in hardship was like a neon sign flashing, "The Holy Spirit has changed these people!" Even though they were experiencing affliction, there was joy! Wouldn't that be a great motto for life? "In much affliction, joy!"

> Their joy in hardship was like a flashing neon sign.

This is crucial to our understanding of the Christian life. At the very outset of their Christian lives, Paul did not say to these Thessalonians, *If you become a Christian, then there will be no more affliction.* There are some people today who teach that if you become a Christian, you will know no more affliction—and so if you do have affliction, it's because you don't have enough faith. No: when the Holy Spirit comes with power, it does not mean no affliction; it means affliction with joy.

This was the life that Paul lived: "I am filling up what is lacking in Christ's afflictions for the sake of his body, that is, the church" (Colossians 1:24). This was the life that Paul called others to live: a life that even embraced affliction for the sake of Christ and the church. So in our lives, afflictions ought to be the last thing to surprise us.

Everybody in this life has afflictions; not everybody has joy. And Christian joy is a specific kind of joy—"the joy of the Holy Spirit." This is a joy that does not wither in the soil of hardship—in fact, oftentimes it blooms—because the Spirit-filled believer knows that suffering can take nothing from them that they truly need. It is a joy that survives even if our world has been turned inside out and upside down. And since it is only the Spirit who can give such joy, Paul knew that these Thessalonians had really been converted. He knew that God had really come in power with the gospel because, in their afflictions, these new Christians continued to display an evident, manifest joy.

The last time I was preaching through 1 Thessalonians, the brother of one of our **ruling elders** was diagnosed with an aggressive, inoperable cancer. He was a young man, and he was given just weeks to live. I called up our elder, just to check on him—and fifteen minutes after he picked up the phone, I had received from him fifteen minutes of more encouragement than I can ever remember. I said to him, "Friend, I want you to remember every word you just said to me, because if I ever get that kind of diagnosis one day, I'm calling you up, and I want you to say it to me."

What was going on in that phone call was this: in the midst of losing a brother he loved, that believer had articulated joy in the Holy Spirit. And that's what Paul is speaking of here. He looked at the lives of the Thessalonians, and he saw that in the midst of all their afflictions there was an inextinguishable joy that only the Holy Spirit could have put there.

In this life, we will suffer afflictions. Some will come because we are Christians living in a **fallen world**; others simply because we are people living in a fallen world. Our faith does not render us immune from such pain; it does not mean that the pain is not real or that we won't feel it. But it does bring us joy in such pain, alongside the sorrow. Whatever we lose, we cannot lose Christ, and so we cannot lose salvation. Our afflictions will be hard—sometimes very hard indeed. But they need not touch our faith, our love, or our hope. If you are living through affliction of some manner today, you have an opportunity to testify to the power of the gospel. Let that gospel be your joy in those afflictions. You are not called to have joy *about* those afflictions (we are not masochists)—but you are invited and called to know joy *in* them because of the Holy Spirit.

May people look at us and know that the kind of joy we display is inexplicable from our circumstances, and may they ask us for the reason for the hope that we have, that we might be able to speak to them of the gospel.

Questions for reflection

1. Paul begins his letter with encouragement before moving on to exhortations and instructions. Why? How can we imitate this in our own relationships?

2. "The Holy Spirit ... comes to convert, and he comes to sanctify" (p 23). How have you seen the Holy Spirit at work in your own life? What do you long for him to do in you next?

3. Think about the situations you are facing in the coming week. What opportunities might you have to share the gospel? What opportunities might you have to live in a way that demonstrates the gospel's power?

2. A GODLY REPUTATION

Paul has been encouraging the Thessalonians by telling them what he sees God doing in their midst, and what he is therefore giving thanks to God for. **Verses 6-10** contain one further specific aspect of his thanksgiving.

In **verse 6**, Paul commends the Thessalonians for the way they have imitated him, and, in doing so, have imitated their Lord; and for the way they have joyfully received and obeyed the word as it came to them, even though it has brought suffering. **Verses 7-8** describe the change that the gospel has worked in them—and it's a change that has led them to gain a reputation among the other Christians and even the surrounding community, in their own region and beyond.

This was a church whose reputation preceded them—and it was a godly reputation. Paul would start to tell people about this church, and the people would say, *We've already heard about them*. If we would have our churches enjoy a similar reputation, then we will need to learn three things that Paul explores in **verses 6-10**. First of all, the way that the gospel is made visible in the church. Second, what **conversion** entails. And then third, the life that converted believers in the church live in light of the gospel.

Making the Gospel Visible

Verses 7-8 can be summarized by a little sentence that is big with truth: the church makes the gospel visible. Of course, we have already seen that the gospel is shared through words. As Paul says in Romans 10:17, "Faith comes from hearing." But the gospel does not merely come in words; it comes with power (1 Thessalonians 1:5), and it results in transformed lives. And so, in the church, we are meant to see the glorious effect of the gospel at work in people's lives.

In that sense, the church makes the gospel visible. In the church, the power of the gospel, in how it transforms us, is displayed to others. The way people know that these Christians in Thessalonica aren't just talking—the way it becomes clear that what they're talking about has validity and reality—is by the dramatic change that results in them from believing the gospel. In a congregation, the glorious reality created by the Holy Spirit in the gospel is manifested to the watching world.

Paul catalogs how that happened among the Thessalonians in six steps.

1. *They became imitators of Paul and his mission team (**v 6**).* Have you ever been around a Christian and found yourself thinking, "When I grow up, I want to be a Christian like him; I want to be a Christian like her"? We all need to be around Christians like that from time to time. They so manifest the reality of the gospel that they motivate us to be more like Christ. When we see how the gospel changes people, we ourselves want to become more like gospel-soaked people. And Paul says that's exactly what happened with the Thessalonians. After Paul and his church-planting team came in—and they were only there for three weeks (Acts 17:1-2)—suddenly people who had been pagans were saying, *I want to live like that. I want to be like them. I want my life to look like their lives look.*

   Paul says in 1 Thessalonians 1:5, "You know what kind of men we proved to be among you for your sake." We can get an insight into "what kind of men" Paul and his companions were in the book of Acts. They were obedient. Called by God to preach the gospel in the region of Macedonia, where Thessalonica was situated, they went there at once (Acts 16:9-10). Paul was consistent:

he preached about Jesus in the synagogue in Thessalonica on three successive **Sabbaths** (17:1-3). Paul did not show favoritism: he preached to both Jews and Gentiles (v 4). Paul was not afraid: his preaching had landed him in prison in Philippi, another town in the region, and yet he carried on. Sure enough, his preaching caused a riot in Thessalonica (v 5)—and it was local believers who ended up being arrested (v 6-7). In that sense, they were already imitating Paul!

2. *They became imitators of the Lord (1 Thessalonians **1:6**).* Of course, Jesus is not just an example to us. The gospel is not "Jesus has set a good example—now you go and be good." If that's the gospel, we're all in trouble. The gospel is about what Jesus has done for us that we could not do and would not do for ourselves. But having declared the glorious truth of Jesus and his person and work, so often Paul and the other writers of the New Testament encourage us to follow Jesus' example. So, for instance, when Paul encourages the Philippians not to be selfish and prideful but to be humble, he says, "Have this mind among yourselves, which is yours in Christ Jesus" (Philippians 2:5). Paul reminds the Corinthians that "though [Jesus] was rich, yet for your sake he became poor, so that you by his poverty might become rich" (2 Corinthians 8:9)—and he says that in order to encourage the Corinthians to be generous in their giving. Over and over in the New Testament, we can see Paul and the other writers pointing to Jesus as their example and encouraging believers to follow specific aspects of his behavior. And this is what the Thessalonian Christians have done.

3. *They "received the word in much affliction" (1 Thessalonians **1:6**).* As we saw in the previous chapter, even though becoming Christians cost them dearly—they were persecuted and afflicted because they received the word—they kept believing. They didn't believe the gospel because it meant Easy Street for them. They believed the gospel even though it came served with affliction.

4. Not only that, but *they received the word in affliction with joy.* In a sense, this is a subset of their imitation of Paul and the Lord, because to do this is to be just like Paul and Jesus. Remember Paul and Silas in the Philippian jail: they were awaiting arraignment and what were they doing at midnight? They were singing hymns (Acts 16:22-25)! Is that not a picture of trusting God through affliction with joy? And who is that like? Jesus. As the author of the letter to the Hebrews says, our Lord Jesus Christ "endured the cross, despising the shame." Why? "For the *joy* set before him" (Hebrews 12:2, my emphasis).

5. All this had the result that *"you became an example"* (1 Thessalonians *1:7*). These new Christians followed the example of Paul, his companions, and supremely the Lord Jesus—and look what happened! Other Christians started saying, *We want to be like them!* Here's the chain: they saw Paul and they said, *We want to be like him.* They heard about Jesus and they said, *We want to be like him.* And now other Christians see them and they say, *We want to be like them.* They went from being imitators to being examples (or rather, to both imitators *and* examples).

6. Now, *they have a growing good reputation (v 8).* "Not only has the word of the Lord sounded forth from you in Macedonia and Achaia, but your faith in God has gone forth everywhere, so that we need not say anything." Paul is not saying that he doesn't need to preach the gospel anymore because the reputation of the Thessalonian church on its own is sufficient to save. He's saying that he can hardly go anywhere in the region and tell the story of his time in Thessalonica without someone saying, *I've already heard about that, Paul.* And so the conduct of these new Christians has opened the door for fruitful gospel witness. Now people know that the gospel comes with power, producing a dramatic transformation. They know this because they have seen it in the Thessalonian church.

Do They Say Something?

All this means that we need to ask ourselves the question: what would people who live around my church say about my church? Would they look at our lives—at my life—and see that the gospel produces dramatic change? Could Paul commend and encourage your church in the way he could the Thessalonian church? Is the gospel being made visible in your church, through the transformation it has produced and is producing in people's lives?

I remember a conversation that my friend Mark Dever, the **pastor** at Capitol Hill Baptist Church in Washington, D.C., told me of several years ago. He was talking with a **Baptist** pastor in a small town of four or five thousand, somewhere in the South. In the course of the conversation, this pastor said to Mark, "We've had 200 **baptisms** at the church in this last year." *Two hundred professions of faith!* Mark responded, "You must have set your town on its ear!" And the pastor replied, "What do you mean? I don't know what you're talking about."

> We should expect real Christians to make the gospel visible.

And Mark said to him, "Wait a second. You've got four or five thousand people in your town. You're telling me that 200 people have been converted to the Lord, and not everybody is talking about it?"

The point is this: real conversion produces real change. We should expect real Christians to make the gospel visible. Mark was saying that if those 200 baptisms represented 200 conversions to Christ in a town of four or five thousand, people would notice it. They would wonder what was happening in that church. That church would enjoy a growing reputation, just as the Thessalonian one did.

So, what do you think they'd say about your church, out there? I am not saying that people should have only good things to say. No doubt there were some in Thessalonica who looked over at this group of their fellow citizens who had converted to Christ and said, *Those people are a bunch of nuts!* I am not asking what slick public relations or marketing campaigns your church runs. I am asking whether the gospel is being made visible in such a way that people notice. Maybe they are drawn to it; maybe they are repelled by it. "We are the aroma of Christ ... to one a fragrance from death to death, to the other a fragrance from life to life" (2 Corinthians 2:15-16). But I am asking: do they notice it because the gospel has made a difference?

That was the case in Thessalonica and in the surrounding region— not just in Macedonia but also in next-door Achaia (both regions are now part of modern-day Greece). Whatever people were saying about the church, they were saying *something*. We need to ask whether we, too, see the gospel being manifested in changed lives—in a change in *our* life.

"Through us [God] spreads the fragrance of the knowledge of him everywhere," says Paul in 2 Corinthians 2:14. But thankfully he then adds, "Who is sufficient for these things?" (v 16). To stretch Paul's metaphor, as Christians, we are walking in a procession, carrying Christ's perfume through the world. We are not asked to be the originators of the perfume—that's Jesus' job. Perhaps you know that you are not as fragrant as you could be; you might even fear that your bottle of perfume is running out or wonder whether you had one in the first place. But Jesus said, "With the measure you use, it will be measured to you" (Mark 4:24). If you are in Christ, the Spirit is at work in you; he will work in you more, if you are willing. Ask the Spirit for a bigger bottle of perfume. Ask him to help you spread that fragrance. Ask him to transform you. And remember that however much you fail, however little scent you spread, it is Jesus who leads you in that procession. He has given you your place there. No amount of failure can take that away.

Questions for reflection

1. Who do you know whose faith and life you want to imitate? What is it about them that you find so attractive? What is one step you could take to become more like them?

2. Read Acts 17:1-9. How could we be imitators of Paul today?

3. How would you answer the questions at the start of the section "Do They Say Something"?

PART TWO

The Essence of Conversion

From 2006 to 2022, every other year in the spring, a group of around 10,000 pastors and church leaders would meet in Louisville, Kentucky at a gathering called "Together for the Gospel." And each time, we focused our talks on the gospel, and we opened or closed some of the sessions with the **testimonies** of Christians who had been dramatically converted and whose lives had been dramatically changed by the power of the gospel.

One of the videos that stays with me still is from one of the earlier T4G gatherings, over a decade ago. It was an account from a young pastor's wife who, along with her husband, was about to take up the charge in a small church in Indiana. She had grown up in Arkansas, and she had lived a life of promiscuity and alcohol and drug abuse. She became pregnant out of wedlock with the man who became her husband. They were involved in the distribution of drugs; on one occasion, they held a drug party at their house with their infant child present. Then a Christian woman shared the gospel with her and persuaded her to come to church. She came to faith in Christ, and then her partner came to faith in Christ, and their lives were dramatically changed. Paul would say that the "gospel came to [them] not only in word, but also in power and in the Holy Spirit" (v 5).

Now this couple are a pastor and pastor's wife, leading a Bible-believing church in Indiana. That's the power of the gospel at work in the lives of people whose lives were a mess but have been dramatically transformed. That's true conversion. That's what Paul is describing in 1 Thessalonians **1:9**. I love how Paul describes conversion here—he gives us a sentence that's one of the best descriptions of conversion that you'll find in all of the New Testament. What happens when conversion takes place in a person's life? He describes it here in this verse:

"They themselves report concerning us the kind of reception
  we had among you, and how you turned to God from idols to
  serve the living and true God."

The New Testament has all sorts of ways to summarize what conversion is. It talks about going from death to life: "You were dead in the trespasses and sins in which you once walked ... But God ... made us alive together with Christ" (Ephesians 2:1-2, 4-5). In the same letter, Paul uses the imagery of light and dark: "At one time you were darkness, but now you are light in the Lord" (5:8). Jesus spoke of the new birth to Nicodemus: "Unless one is born again he cannot see the kingdom of God" (John 3:3). Peter picks up on the same image in 1 Peter 1:3.

Those are all summaries and pictures of what conversion involves. Here in 1 Thessalonians **1:9**, Paul employs another one of them: turning and serving. This is a glorious description of conversion!

In this Thessalonian context, these people really were pagan idolaters, in the sense of bowing down to worship statues at altars or shrines or temples, just as in Athens (see Acts 17:16, 22-23). Paul's choice of phrase indicates that most of this congregation was Gentile; he wouldn't have said this about a Jewish congregation.

These pagan Gentile Thessalonians were idol-worshipers. And then they turned from those idols to the living and the true God. They were converted. That was their story.

Identifying Our Idols

This is our story, too, even if we have not worshiped statues. Idol worship is not restricted to people who are pagan polytheists. All of us struggle with idolatry; it is a foundational sin that all of us fight against or give in to. An idol is anything in which we think we can find ultimate security and satisfaction, instead of or better than in God. We set that thing up as our ultimate source of satisfaction and security. It becomes a god to us, and we worship and serve and sacrifice for it. We all struggle with this, including after we are converted. Conversion involves a decisive turn away from idols to serve the living God; but we also continue to turn away from idols to serve him. The created things that the world loves to worship continue to beckon to God's people, and so there has to be an ongoing turning away from them. That's sanctification.

So could this be said of us: that we have turned from our idols to serve the living and true God, and that we have continued to do so? Have we determined not just to follow the culture around us like lemmings over a cliff? Are we making sure we don't go after the things that everybody else is going after? What would people notice and say about you?

> Have we turned from our idols? Have we determined not to follow the culture around us like lemmings over a cliff?

At this point, I could list some of the idols that Western culture sets before us and that we might be going after. But if I do that, some will read my list and respond by thinking, "Whew, none of those in that list are idols of mine; maybe I don't have a problem with idolatry." It is much more helpful, though far more sobering, to ask yourself three questions that will identify your idols—because we all have them.

The first question is this: *What do I think about? What do I think about when I'm not thinking about anything else?* In those moments when you are frustrated and disappointed by something and you seek escape in your thoughts, you will think about the thing that you believe will give you relief from whatever your frustration and your disappointment is about. Thinking about this thing gives you pleasure; it gives you satisfaction; it gives you security. It might be what you think about right before you fall asleep at night, when you're trying to escape from the problems of the day; or when you're simply dreaming or wishing; when you are fantasizing about something, about someone, about some desire. What do you think about in those quiet moments when you're away from the press of the immediate demands and the fights of the day? What is that thing that you think about that gives you hope and delight? When you begin to identify that thing or those things, you're coming close to identifying your idols.

Here's the second question: *How do I spend my time, my resources, and my energy?* Because when you look at those three things and you ask that question, you're going to see the things that you really care about. I remember sociologists saying 30 years or so ago that a day was going to come when people would value their time more than they valued their money. I thought that was crazy; but I'm seeing more and more of it now. Maybe it's because of the rush of the culture that we're in. Time and resources and energy—those are precious things. We have a finite amount of them, no matter how much we have. And how you use those things indicates what you really value, because typically you spend your time and your resources and your energy on the things that you care about the most and that you believe will deliver you the most. Have a look at your schedule and your bank statement. Look there, and you'll probably be able to identify some of your idols.

And then the third question: *What disappoints me? What absolutely crushes me with disappointment? What, if I lost it or failed at it, would make me feel crushed or worthless?* The chances are that in answering that, you're going to find an idol. There's going to be something that you think that you need to have or something that you desperately want to have that you don't have, and you're disappointed by its lack. It may be a longed-for circumstance that you cannot seem to realize. It may have to do with your family life. It may have to do with your vocation. It may have to do with your children or your parents.

The difference between a converted believer and an unconverted person is not whether we struggle with idolatry—it is what we do when we realize we are struggling. The converted believer has committed to turn away from an idol, however acceptable in our culture or rooted in our heart it may be, and to serve God instead, by trusting him to deliver and satisfy. In this sense, we have turned from our idols to serve the living and true God. It doesn't mean that our battle with idolatry ends, but it should mean that people can tell that we are worshipers of God ultimately, rather than worshipers of anything else. And this described the Thessalonian church, Paul says. When people around them looked at them, they could tell that the believers were no longer idol worshipers. They really believed that God alone was to be worshiped and he was truly the source of their security and satisfaction. Could that be said, more and more, of you, and of your church? We may not have statues in our homes to throw away, but we've all got idols to put away.

Living Life in Light of Jesus' Return

Conversion involves turning and serving and waiting. Paul knows that the Thessalonians are living life in light of Jesus' return; they "wait for [God's] Son from heaven" (1 Thessalonians **1:10**). One of the ways that people saw that the Thessalonians' lives had been changed by the gospel is that they were now living life in light of Jesus' return. They were waiting expectantly for it. Their lives now were changed because of their confident expectation that Jesus was going to come again.

Why could they look forward to it with excitement, rather than trepidation or terror? Because they knew that Jesus is the one "who delivers us from the **wrath** to come" (v 10); that is, they were confident that he would shield them from his own wrath. Revelation 6:15-17 looks forward to the day when...

> "the kings of the earth and the great ones and the generals
> and the rich and the powerful, and everyone, slave and free,
> [will hide] themselves in the caves and among the rocks of the
> mountains, calling to the mountains and rocks, 'Fall on us and
> hide us from the face of him who is seated on the throne, and
> from the wrath of the Lamb, for the great day of their wrath
> has come, and who can stand?'"

Who can stand? These Thessalonians are confident that they will—
that they will not face wrath because the Lamb, Jesus, has borne that
wrath for them. Thus, though they look for a day when God is going
to come and set everything right and punish every sin and bring about
a just judgment of all wickedness, yet they know they are not going
to face that wrath because Jesus has died for them. So they long for
that day, and they wait for it, and they live their lives in light of it. It's
changed their ambitions, it's changed their desires, it's changed their
behaviors, and it's changed their worship. And everyone can see the
difference it has made.

Again, we must ask: would people say that about you and me? The
worst thing that could be said of us is that the gospel does not make
a difference to the way that we live. The greatest encouragement we
can hear, and that we can be, is that the gospel is clearly changing
how we think and love and live. One of the great ways in which we
bear witness to the watching world that the gospel is true is in the
way that the gospel transforms our lives and sets us free from idolatry
to serve the living and true God as we wait for his Son to return and
save us.

So, as Paul encourages these Thessalonians and thanks God for
them, we're seeing what we should aspire to: that we would become
an example to other believers of lives changed utterly because we
have turned from idols, because we are living to serve God, and because we are waiting with confident expectation for the return of the
risen Jesus, the Lamb, who bore his own wrath in our place so that we
might enjoy him forever. Let it be true of us, as it was of those Thessalonian believers, that our loved ones, our friends, our neighbors, our
colleagues at work, would see that the gospel has changed us, and
would say, "I don't know what it is, but something is clearly going on
at that church."

Questions for reflection

1. Consider the questions in the section "Identifying Our Idols". What idols can you identify in your own life?

2. How is Jesus, "the living and true God" (1 Thessalonians 1:9) and the one "who delivers us from the wrath to come" (v 10), better than those things?

3. What will it look like for you to turn away from idols and serve God this week?

3. FAITHFUL MINISTRY

In 1 Thessalonians 2 – 3, Paul defends his **ministry** to the Thessalonian church. It seems that there are people in Thessalonica who are trying to undermine his credibility. So he recounts, describes, and then explains his ministry. He recounts what he did among them, so that they will have to say, *Oh yes, we remember you doing that*. He describes how he did it, so that they will have to say, Oh yes,we remember what your manner was like among us. And he explains what his goal was when he was doing those things, so that they will have to say, *Oh yes, we remember that you did have our best interests at heart*. Then the Thessalonians will conclude that the charges being brought against Paul are clearly untrue.

In this chapter we will look at the first twelve verses of chapter 2. Here's what John Stott says about this passage in particular:

> "Paul's critics took full advantage of his sudden disappearance. In order to undermine his authority and his gospel, they determined to discredit him, so they launched a malicious sneer campaign. By studying Paul's self-defense, it is possible for us to reconstruct their slanders." (*The Message of Thessalonians*, p 45-46)

So as we read, we can be on the lookout for Paul's hints at the accusations he was faced with.

But that is not the only reason to read this passage. In describing and explaining his ministry, Paul is actually providing us with a philosophy of ministry: principles for how it is supposed to be done and why. There is rich material here for reflection on what we're supposed to be doing as we minister in the church of God. This doesn't apply to church leaders only—it applies to anyone who serves in the church in any way.

Slander and Accusation

The first accusation that we can see made against Paul was that his teaching was pointless; that is why he says, "Our coming to you was not in vain" (1 Thessalonians **2:1**). He has already explained the impact that his teaching had among the Thessalonians (1:7-9). Was his coming in vain? No, he is calling them to remember that his teaching had a profound effect on them, and not just on them but on other Christians throughout the whole of Greece.

Second behind **2:2** is the charge that, as soon as the going got tough, Paul got out of town.

What had happened in Thessalonica is told in Acts 17:1-10. A violent mob formed to attack Paul and Silas, and when they could not find them, they seized some of the other believers in Thessalonica and dragged them before the authorities to accuse them. The danger was so great that Paul and Silas were smuggled out of the city, and eventually had to go as far as Athens to escape the Thessalonian Jews who were opposing the gospel.

Somehow, it seems, the Thessalonian believers are now looking back at that and blaming Paul for running away. So in 1 Thessalonians **2:2** Paul points out that he had already been beaten up in Philippi. (The story is told in Acts 16:19-24.) He's saying, *I'm no coward. If I were a guy that didn't want to get beaten up, I would have looked for another line of work.* The accusation that he ran away out of cowardice is a slanderous one. Paul emphasizes this by saying, "We had boldness in our God to declare to you the gospel of God in the midst of much conflict." He came to the Thessalonians knowing that there would be more conflict, just as there had been among the Philippians. He knew that if he proclaimed the gospel in Thessalonica, he would probably get beaten up again; but nevertheless, he came in boldness.

1 Thessalonians **2:3** shows us a third accusation. "Our appeal does not spring from error or impurity or any attempt to deceive." What were they saying about him? That what he taught was in error, that it sprang from his own immorality, and that his intention was to deceive the Thessalonians.

For now, Paul simply says that this accusation is not true. In the rest of chapters 2 and 3, he will demonstrate what his appeal to the Thessalonians really sprang from. His response is *Actually, no, what we taught you was true. It didn't spring from base motives. It actually sprang from a heart that had been changed by the grace of God. I didn't intend to deceive you. In fact, I said some things to you that I knew you weren't going to like hearing; but they were true, and so I told them to you anyway.*

Stott sums up what people in Thessalonica were saying about Paul this way:

> "He ran away … and hasn't been seen or heard since! Obviously he's insincere, impelled by the basest motives. He's just one of those many phoney teachers who tramp up and down the Egnatian Way. In a word, he's a charlatan. He's in his job only for what he can get out of it in terms of money, prestige or power. So when opposition arose, and he found himself in personal danger, he took to his heels and ran! He doesn't care about you Thessalonian disciples of his; he has abandoned you! He's much more concerned about his own skin than your welfare."
>
> (*The Message of Thessalonians*, p 46)

These accusations are one reason why Paul wrote these verses: to patiently explain and defend himself with the truth. But here's the beautiful thing—in the course of Paul's defense, he actually describes for us what faithful gospel ministry looks like.

Entrusted by God

It's not enough for Paul to simply assert that his ministry is not self-seeking. He wants the Thessalonian Christians to know where his motivation really lies. He starts by explaining that it comes from the Lord: "We have been approved by God to be entrusted with the gospel" (**v 4**).

This is not the only time that Paul reminds his readers of his special position as one specifically sent out by God. He often introduces himself this way at the start of his letters: "Paul ... called to be an apostle" (Romans 1:1; 1 Corinthians 1:1; Galatians 1:1; 1 Timothy 2:7). The point is not to make sure that everybody knows how important Paul is; it's to make sure that everybody knows that his message doesn't come from himself. He has been sent—that's what the word "apostle" means. That is the foundation of his ministry.

In Acts 26 we hear Paul telling the full story of his calling. Blinded by a light from heaven on his way to Damascus, Paul heard the voice of Jesus: "I have appeared to you for this purpose, to appoint you as a servant and witness ... to open [people's] eyes, so that they may turn from darkness to light and from the power of Satan to God" (Acts 26:16, 18). What a calling! And it was not something Paul was going to forget in a hurry. That moment on the Damascus road was what drove him through the rest of his life. He had been entrusted with this message of salvation, and he was not going to stop proclaiming it.

> Our message is a deposit, a precious treasure. It needs to be carefully guarded and eagerly passed on.

In 1 Timothy Paul uses language similar to 1 Thessalonians 2:4 to describe the teaching of Timothy, a younger pastor: "O Timothy, guard the deposit entrusted to you" (1 Timothy 6:20). This message is a "deposit," a precious treasure entrusted to Timothy, to Paul, and to other teachers of God's word. It needs to be carefully guarded—in the sense of not allowing it to be compromised or added to with other teaching that doesn't come from Christ—and eagerly passed on. The same is true for us today. Not all are preachers or teachers like Paul and Timothy, but all of us have been entrusted with the truth. How will we treat this precious deposit?

Paul is an example to us. To him, the message Jesus has entrusted him with is the most important thing in his life. He takes his mission seriously—not only because it comes from God but because he can please God by it. "We speak, not to please man, but to please God who tests our hearts" (1 Thessalonians **2:4**). This doesn't mean that God is waiting to pounce when Paul slips up, like a driving examiner ready to spot the smallest error. No, God is delighted by what Paul is doing, and that's a huge motivator for Paul.

Imagine a young girl who takes dancing lessons. One day it's her turn to perform in front of the class. When she gets on stage to dance, who is she seeking to please? Her teacher. She has been taught and trained by this teacher, and she wants to dance in just the way she's been trained to. She is going to feel the teacher's pleasure when she performs well. Of course, she also wants to please and delight the rest of the audience—but ultimately it's only one person's opinion that really matters.

This is what Paul means when he says he speaks to please God, not man. Hopefully, his words *will* please the men and women who hear him: his goal, after all, is that they will hear the truth and be transformed. But it is God's opinion that matters most. God is the best judge of what Paul says because it all comes from him.

It is so tempting, in ministry and in all of life, to say what other people want us to say. It's hard to stand up for the truth when the truth is awkward or painful or difficult to hear. When we're proclaiming the gospel, it's particularly tempting to leave out the parts about God's judgment and his wrath against sin. But it's God's opinion we've got to trust. He sees our hearts, and he is deeply pleased when we look to him, not anyone else, to decide what to say.

What does this look like in practice? In **verses 5-6** Paul highlights three things which he didn't do—three things which would constitute seeking to please man instead of God.

1. No words of flattery—that is, Paul never sought to curry favor but relied on speaking the truth.

2. No pretext for greed—that is, Paul never used his preaching as a cover for getting money out of people.

3. No seeking glory—that is, Paul never tried to be the center or the focus of his preaching but always deflected attention onto Jesus.

Paul's position as an apostle was a special one, but he never abused it (**v 6**). He sought to make himself low so that no one could accuse him of self-promotion or self-seeking. This is an immense challenge for us today—whatever our position in the church. It's so easy to want people to admire and look up to us; it's so tempting to think that we should be rewarded for our service. But Paul calls us to have the same mindset that was in Christ Jesus:

"… who, though he was in the form of God, did not count equality with God a thing to be grasped, but emptied himself, by taking the form of a servant, being born in the likeness of men. And being found in human form, he humbled himself by becoming obedient to the point of death, even death on a cross." (Philippians 2:6-8)

Paul's next few verses in 1 Thessalonians explore what such self-emptying and servant-heartedness look like in a church context.

Questions for reflection

1. How can we learn from Paul's description of his ministry? What is one thing you'd like to be true of you in your own ministry?

2. Why is it so tempting to make demands of those we are ministering to, or to flatter them? Which of those is the greater temptation for you?

3. "It's only one person's opinion that really matters." What difference will it make to you to remember this?

PART TWO

I wonder what drives the way you behave with other people in your church. Are you just there to enjoy yourself, or do you take time to think about the impact of your behavior and your words on those around you? In 1 Thessalonians **2:7-12** Paul describes how he behaved with the Thessalonians, and why. He did enjoy being with them—he talks of himself as "affectionately desirous" of them (**v 8**), just like we all are with our close friends. But there was more to this relationship than that. Paul's relationship with the Thessalonian Christians involved enjoyment, delight, and committed friendship, but it also had a purpose.

A Faithful Mother

It may be surprising to hear Paul compare himself to a mother in **verse 7**. We may be used to thinking of Paul as a hard, uncompromising man. After all, he endured so much and remained so committed to the task God had given him. We might expect him to be a harsh taskmaster to others, tolerating no slip-up and brooking no disagreement. But that is not the picture of him we see here in **verses 7-8**. Here Paul describes himself and his companions as gentle, affectionate, and full of love.

The image of a "nursing mother" is a powerful one, and very specific. This is not just any mother. A nursing mother is one who is breastfeeding a small baby. During the first few weeks of a baby's life, he or she demands milk at least eight times a day. That's at least every three hours. And does the mother leave the baby alone in between feeds? No—she cuddles him, plays with him, talks to him. She gets up in the middle of the night to comfort him. She doesn't leave others to look after him—Paul describes her as "taking care of her own children."

This image is one of total, 24-hour commitment. In **verse 8** Paul adds that "we were ready to share with you not only the gospel of

God but also our own selves." Isn't that like a mother with a small child? In those early days and weeks, everything in her life revolves around her baby. She gives herself in every way: physically, mentally, and emotionally. When a couple becomes parents, everything changes to make room for this new addition to their family. For Paul, these new Christians are not like a new set of employees that he has to train, or even new friends that he wants to be kind to. They are like his children. "You had become very dear to us," he acknowledges (**v 8**). When these Thessalonians became Christians, it was not just their lives that changed—Paul's did too.

This is what faithful ministry looks like. Faithfulness to God comes first. But faithfulness to those you are ministering to comes a close second. Paul, like Jesus, was ready to empty himself for the sake of these new disciples whom he loved. He was as gentle, as affectionate, and as committed as a nursing mother taking care of her children. He did not let them down. He did not speak harshly or impatiently to them. He put their needs above his own. This is our goal as ministers of the gospel and members of the church. Make no mistake, it's a very high goal, and we need the Spirit's help.

A Blameless Worker

As if Paul's words in **verses 7-8** weren't challenging enough, in **verses 9-10** he raises the bar of faithful ministry even more. He is now not just talking about his love for the Thessalonians but his conduct throughout his stay with them. Being a faithful minister of the gospel involves blameless conduct.

Paul has already told us that he did not come "with a pretext for greed" (**v 5**). In **verse 9** he expands on that by reminding the Thessalonians that "we worked night and day, that we might not be a burden to any of you." In other words, Paul and his companions worked to support themselves financially so that the fledgling Christians in Thessalonica did not have to support them. In 1 Corinthians 9 Paul explains why this was his practice. He argues that in fact he does have a right to be paid for his ministry (v 11, 14—which is why we pay our church pastors today). Then he adds, "Nevertheless, we have not made use of this right, but we endure anything rather than put an obstacle in the way of the gospel of Christ" (v 12).

Why would being paid for ministry put an obstacle in the way of the gospel? Presumably because of the very accusations Paul is dealing with in 1 Thessalonians 2. If people can accuse him of taking advantage of others financially, there will be some who will doubt his message. Paul wants to be beyond blameless; not only is his own conscience satisfied, but no one else can even accuse him of wrongdoing. This is why Paul adds in 1 Thessalonians **2:10**, "You are witnesses, and God also, how holy and righteous and blameless was our conduct toward you believers." Paul's behavior was above reproach.

This doesn't mean that Paul was without sin. Of course he sinned; all of us do. But he knows that in these matters he has been living as God would have him live. He even calls God as a witness of this (**v 10**). What empowered Paul to live this way? The gospel of God (**v 9**). Paul was so passionately convinced of the worth of preaching the good news of Jesus Christ that he was able to bring his behavior in line with it. This is a lesson to us. The more we reflect on the good news, the more we internalize it, and the more we prioritize it, the more holy and righteous and blameless our conduct will be.

Walk in a Manner Worthy

In **verse 12** Paul finally declares the purpose of all his motherly love and blameless conduct. All of it was in the hope that the Thessalonian Christians will "walk in a manner worthy of God, who calls you into his own kingdom and glory."

This idea of living a life that is fitting is all over the writings of the apostle Paul. Several times he uses walking as a metaphor for living (see Ephesians 4:1; Colossians 1:10). The Christian life is a journey. We're on a pilgrimage, taking a long walk together. And there is a way to walk that is worthy of the calling of God on our lives. The same ideas come up in Philippians 1:27 and 2 Thessalonians 1:5, 11. Throughout his letters, Paul is clearly setting very lofty goals for our Christian behavior.

What does it mean to live a life worthy of the God who has called us, or worthy of the gospel of the Lord Jesus Christ? It means to live in such a way that our living fits what we believe, what we have been called for, and who has called us. People should look at what we say we believe and at the way we live and say, "Yes, those go together. There's no hypocrisy there. These are people who are living out sincerely what they believe." We are to live Christianly.

Paul has already described what that looked like in his own life. Now we see that this was his purpose. His own walk was designed to influence the Thessalonians' walk—and ours too. Fortunately for us, living Christianly is not just a matter of trying our hardest to be like Paul. We cannot manage that in our own strength! But two words that Paul uses at the end of 1 Thessalonians **2:12** hint at *how* we can begin to walk in a manner worthy of God. What motivates us, and what empowers us? It's all about God's kingdom and God's glory.

Called into God's Kingdom

First, we are to live in a manner that is worthy of the God who has called us into his kingdom. The idea here is that we live life knowing who our King is. We've been called out of this world and into God's kingdom. Knowing that Jesus is our King is what frees us to live for him and not for the world.

The difference between the two was perhaps especially stark in Paul's time. In the eastern parts of the Roman world, the emperor was worshiped as a god. At various civil public ceremonies, sacrifices would be offered to the living spirit of the emperor. But because Christians believed that there is only one King, who is God—the Lord Jesus Christ, who is the King of his church—they would not participate in those ceremonies. And that did not go down well with their neighbors or the ruling authorities.

Think of it this way. In America, the last Monday in May is Memorial Day, when beautiful tributes are made to the fallen soldiers, sailors, airmen, and marines who have given their lives so that we can live in freedom. In the UK and Commonwealth countries, the equivalent is Remembrance Day on November 11th. These are special, solemn, unifying days. What if, as Christians, we refused to participate? What would people say about us? They'd say, "You're not patriotic! You don't love your country! You don't appreciate the sacrifices that people have made for you!"

That is something like what the Thessalonian believers faced; and they faced it because (unlike on Memorial Day) participating in those ceremonies would have required them to worship a god who is not God and a king who was not their King. Because they believed that they had been called into God's kingdom, they refused to go along with their culture and worship Caesar. And it brought them persecution.

We don't face that today, exactly; but persecution is happening as Christians refuse to let anyone other than Jesus be their King. A few years back I spent some time with a faithful pastor named John Yates. In 2006, the members of John's church voted to leave the **Episcopal Church** after it **ordained** an openly practicing homosexual bishop. The result was that the Episcopal diocese disputed the ownership of their church building, and a few years later John's congregation was turned out. John Yates and his congregation walked away from the building they had called home for so many years. Why? Because they were not going to have any other rule but the word of God directing how they did ministry and what they preached and proclaimed. John told me, "I counted it a privilege to be able to lose something dear to me for my Lord."

That short conversation with John filled me up the whole week long, and it encourages me still. Here was a believer with joy in his heart and with bold firmness of purpose and principle who refused to let anybody who denied the final authority of God's word tell him how to live and minister. He knew who his King was.

Of course, most of the fights that we must fight do not involve somebody from the outside telling us to compromise on our obedience to Christ. Mostly such voices come from the inside and involve us ourselves saying we want to be king of our own lives. The things the Lord calls us to do are often hard; they hurt, and we don't like them. The temptation is to say, "Well, I'm the exception to the rule. I don't have to do that. I want to be my own king." Instead we need to resist our own sinful nature and, with the help of God's Spirit, seek to live with Christ as our King—every day of the week, not just on Sundays; in every place we go to, not just the church building; and with every person we meet, not just those who are easy to deal with.

> We need to live with Christ as our King— every day of the week.

In every aspect of life we must say, "God is my King, and therefore I'm going to follow him." It's when we remember this that we will find ourselves living in a manner worthy of Jesus Christ.

Called into God's Glory

Second, Paul encourages us in **verse 12** to "walk in a manner worthy of God, who calls us into his own glory."

Paul mentioned the word "glory" a few verses earlier, in **verse 6**: "Nor did we seek glory from people, whether from you or from others." The word "glory" clearly means prestige, power, or influence. Here, in **verse 12**, Paul picks up the word "glory" again and shows *why* he was not seeking to get glory out of the Thessalonians: because he already had the glory of God.

Paul knew that the glory of God could be known in the face of Jesus Christ (2 Corinthians 4:6), and that when we behold that face, we ourselves are transformed from one degree of glory to another (2 Corinthians 3:18). He knew that although this life involves being afflicted, crushed, perplexed, and persecuted—though "our outer self is wasting away" and does not seem glorious at all—it is also true that in Christ we are being renewed day by day, prepared for the ultimate "glory beyond all comparison" that it will be to behold Christ fully in heaven (2 Corinthians 4:8-9, 16-17). Paul lived knowing where his glory was.

So must we. That is, we have to know where our real treasure in life is. Is it getting what you want, when you want it, how you want it? Or is it knowing God and living in line with all he has called you into? If you're looking for glory in this world from people, you'll end up worshiping something in this world alongside God, or even worshiping someone or something more than you worship God. But if you're looking for the glory that is in God, you'll worship him alone. The Christian life may not feel glorious right now, but in fact it is far more glorious than anything this world offers. If you are in Christ, then you are already being transformed from one degree of glory to another. When you treasure God's glory above all else, then you will live a life worthy of the God who has called you.

Questions for reflection

1. What would it look like for you to be like a faithful mother toward others in your church?

2. What is your greatest hope for those around you? How would it change your behavior if you focused more on helping others to "walk in a manner worthy of God"?

3. When is it most difficult to act in a way that shows that Jesus is our King? How does this passage encourage and equip you to do that?

4. CONSTANT GRATITUDE

Paul has spoken about his desire for how the Thessalonians should behave in the light of the faith they have received. Now, in **verses 13-16**, Paul recounts three specific reasons why he is grateful for what God is already doing by his Spirit in the hearts of the Thessalonians.

Grateful?

What role does gratitude play in your Christian life? I don't just mean gratitude for the earthly blessings that God gives us: the resources that he puts into our hands, the food that he puts into our mouths, the clothes that he puts on our backs, and the roofs that he puts over our heads. Great as those blessings are—and we ought to be grateful for them—I'm especially thinking of gratitude for other people: a gratitude that is regularly looking around and thanking God for what he is doing in the lives of our brothers and sisters in Christ.

Do you find yourself looking around at your circle of Christian friends and at the people in your church regularly and saying, "Lord, I want to thank you for how you are at work in the life of that sister, that brother, in Christ"? Do you find yourself being blessed when you see God's word at work in somebody else's life? Paul is giving us an example of this kind of gratitude here.

This is not the first time that Paul has expressed gratitude or thanksgiving. We've already seen that he actually begins this whole letter by speaking of his gratitude for what God is doing in the Thessalonians (1:2). In verse 5, he was thankful to God that the gospel didn't just come with words but also with power in the lives of the Thessalonians, changing their lives so that they displayed faith and love and hope. Then in verse 6, he was thankful God that even in the midst of affliction they showed joy in Christ.

Here in chapter 2, the same themes pop up again. There are two things Paul specially draws to our attention: first, in **2:13**, what the word of God was doing in the Thessalonians; and then, in **verses 14-16**, how they had become imitators of the churches in Judea in enduring affliction and still believing.

The Word of God at Work

Paul is thankful for two things with regard to the Thessalonians in **verse 13**: both for their receiving of the word of God and for the activity of the word of God in them.

The first thing that Paul wants to thank God for is that the Thessalonians accepted the gospel message "not as the word of men but as what it really is, the word of God." They understood that the gospel was not something that had come out of Paul's own brain—a message that human beings had made up—but was the very word of God.

J.I. Packer says that preaching is "the event of God bringing to an audience a Bible-based, Christ-related, life-impacting message of instruction from himself through the words of a spokesperson" ("Some Perspectives on Preaching," *Ashland Theological Journal*, 1990, p 42-43). That is a wonderful definition. Packer doesn't say that a preacher brings a message about God. He says that God brings a message through a preacher.

We need to understand that every time a church gathers under God's word, the congregation is there to experience a word-mediated encounter between their souls and the living God. God himself is using the preacher as an instrument, as a tool, so that he can speak into each life. That's why it is impossible for us to have too high a view of preaching.

Paul is saying here that the Thessalonians had grasped that. They understood that when he preached the gospel, he had not invented it but received it. This was a message that was given to him by God. This was a message that was being preached *through* him. And he is thanking God that they understand that.

Sometimes at a church service you can see someone grasp this for the very first time. The light has just gone on for them: "This isn't just the words of men; this is the very word of God speaking to me." It's good practice to ask the people around you after the church service, "How did God speak to you through his word today?" Then you will have an opportunity to pause and say, "Lord, thank you that that's your Spirit working in my brother's or sister's life, because they have received the word of God for what it is—your own word!"

Second, Paul is thankful that this word "is at work in you believers."

This is not a dead word; it's a living word. It's a word at work in you. Back in 1:3 he mentioned faith, love, and hope as evidence that God's word is at work in the Thessalonians. It's God's word at work in them causing them to have faith; therefore they are working out that faith. It's God's word at work causing them to have love; therefore they are laboring hard for each other. And it's God's word at work causing them to have hope; therefore they are persevering and enduring. The word of God is transforming the Thessalonians' lives. Paul is looking at that and saying, *Lord, I want to stop right now, and I want to thank you because I see your word at work in them.*

I remember C.J. Mahaney once saying, "If we fail to notice evidence of God's grace in our church, we will gradually become grumblers rather than grateful." A local church is sinners living in close proximity with sinners, and there are things that we will do to make one another grumpy. So if we don't pause from time to time to thank God for those spiritual, gospel things that he is doing in the lives of our brothers and sisters in Christ, we will become grumblers.

In order to actively cultivate gratitude to God for the evidence that he is at work in the hearts of our fellow believers, our eyes have to be open all the time and we need continually to be asking, "What is the Lord doing here?" That's what Paul is pausing to do here, and he's giving us an example. May God enable us to cultivate that kind of gospel gratitude in our own lives.

Imitators of Faithful Churches

In **verse 14**, Paul explains more about what it means that the word of God is at work in the Thessalonian Christians: it is enabling them to believe, even in the midst of persecution. He commends the Thessalonians for becoming "imitators of the churches of God in Jesus Christ that are in Judea." Specifically, they are imitators in the sense of continuing to believe and trust the Lord even while they're experiencing affliction and opposition and persecution.

Paul is pausing to acknowledge this: *I am watching Christians be willing to suffer for Christ and still believe in him and in the gospel.*

Can you look around and see people experiencing affliction because of the gospel of the Lord Jesus Christ? If you can't think of anyone, you're not really looking! It is happening all the time. The person whose family disapproves of them because they prioritize generosity over worldly gain. The person who loses out professionally because they refuse to compromise their integrity. The couple who are run off their feet because they know they have been called to be hospitable and serve the needy. And those are just small-scale examples. Beyond our own Western culture, we all know that missionaries and Christians in many other countries face persecution and difficulty constantly.

> If we don't see faith in affliction as a reason to praise God, we're missing the point.

We may pray for such people and ask God to help them in their sufferings, and that's good; but if we don't see their faith in affliction as a reason to give God praise and thanks, we're missing the point. Paul looks at these Thessalonians experiencing persecution for the sake of the gospel and he says, *Lord, thank you that the gospel is so real in their lives that they're willing to bleed for it.* Affliction is not itself a reason to thank God, but the faith of our brothers and sisters who are suffering and serving is a wonderful reason to thank God for the way he as at work.

The Source of Suffering

The Thessalonians have endured afflictions from their own country-men, just as the Jewish Christians in Judea were enduring afflictions from their countrymen, the Jews (**v 14**). So, in **verses 15-16** Paul explains that the Jews have killed Jesus and the prophets, driven out the apostles, displeased God, opposed all mankind, and hindered the spread of the gospel; and then he says that God's wrath has come down on them.

Very sadly, this passage has sometimes been interpreted as anti-Semitic. Anti-Semitism means suspicion, hatred, or discrimination to-ward Jewish people simply because of their ethnicity and their heri-tage. It is a very, very serious charge. So we need to be totally clear that biblical Christianity emphatically rejects anti-Semitism and holds it to be a grave sin. It is important to bear in mind that Paul was Jewish himself, as was Jesus, and that Paul had a deep and evident love for the Jewish people. In Romans 9:3, Paul says he wishes that God would eternally damn him if that meant he would save his fellow Jews. I have to say, I don't find myself praying that way for anyone! But Paul had that kind of love for the Jews. This was not a man who hated Jewish people, but rather one who loved Jewish people tenaciously. For Paul, they are him and he is them.

This is all the more true because everything that he denounces Israel for doing in 1 Thessalonians 2:**14-16**, Paul has done himself. **Verse 15** says that the Jews "killed both the Lord Jesus and the prophets, and drove us out, and displease God." Paul did not kill Jesus Christ, but did he persecute him? Yes. That is why Jesus said to him (using his pre-Christian name of Saul) on the road to Damascus, "Saul, Saul, why are you persecuting *me*?" (Acts 9:4, my italics). Moreover, Paul/Saul participated in the killing of the prophets, holding the cloaks for the men who stoned **Stephen** to death (Acts 7:58) and approving of the murder (8:1). 1 Thessalonians **2:16** says that the Jews were "hindering [Paul] from speaking to the Gentiles that they might be saved." Paul himself had done exactly the same thing: with every breath in his being he worked to hinder the spread of the gospel (Acts 8:3; 26:9-11).

1 Thessalonians **2:15-16** does not stem from hatred for the Jewish people because of their heritage. This is a condemnation of unbelief and sin—including Paul's own unbelief and sin. Paul isn't talking about all Jews here, as if to be Jewish is to be sinful and face wrath. He is observing the terrible things that have been done by certain Jews.

Verse 14 bears repeating: "You suffered the same things from your own countrymen as they did from the Jews." The Thessalonians have suffered as much from Gentiles as the Jewish Christians in Judea have suffered from the Jews. Both Gentiles and Jews have persecuted God's people. It's also true that both Gentiles and Jews have come into God's people through faith in Christ and then faced persecution.

Paul is therefore doing here exactly what the Old Testament prophets did. They continually denounced Israel for unbelief and sin. Like them, Paul is lamenting the fact that many of his countrymen have not believed God's word and have resisted God's gospel. He is speaking out of love, and most of all out of love for God's word and sadness that it should be disobeyed.

When Paul says that "wrath has come upon them at last" (v 16), it sounds like he is implying that some great catastrophe has hit the Jewish nation. Some interpreters have seen this as a prophecy of the destruction of the temple by the Romans in AD 70, around 20 years after Paul wrote this letter. But why does Paul say wrath has *already* come? Perhaps because the rejection of Jesus was the final nail in the coffin, sealing their fate. In Luke 19:41-44, Jesus himself predicted the invasion of Jerusalem and the destruction of the temple. Why did he say it would happen? "Because you did not know the time of your visitation" (v 44). The Jews of Jesus' time refused to recognize their own Messiah. As a result, God turned them over to wrath.

In Romans 1 – 3, Paul argues that the whole world—that is both Jews and Gentiles—stands condemned by God and is under his just judgment because of sin. This reads like an elaboration on 1 Thessalonians **2:14-16**. All, both Jews and Gentiles, are under sin and deserve wrath. It is a sobering passage to read. Yet, as Paul concludes, he affirms that in Christ there is hope—and this hope is for everyone, both Jew and Gentile. Why?

"[Because] now the righteousness of God has been manifested apart from the law, although the Law and the Prophets bear witness to it—the righteousness of God through faith in Jesus Christ for all who believe. For there is no distinction: for all have sinned and fall short of the glory of God, and are justified by his grace as a gift, through the redemption that is in Christ Jesus." (Romans 3:21-24)

Questions for reflection

1. When we remember that the Bible is the word of God, how should that shape our attitude and approach to sermons, group studies and private Bible-reading?

2. What are you most grateful for in your church today?

3. How do 1 Thessalonians 2:15-16 and Romans 3:21-24 make you feel about your own sin and about the redemption you've been offered?

PART TWO

In the final four verses of chapter 2, Paul returns to his response to the detractors in Thessalonica who are slandering him. He does so by expressing his love for these Christians. So we get a picture of how a pastor loves his people. But along the way, Paul also tells us two things that are very important about living life in the light of Jesus' return. He acknowledges the power of Satan working against him (1 Thessalonians **2:18**), and then he expresses what the ultimate reward is for gospel ministry (**v 19-20**).

A Pastor's Love

It seems that people are saying things to the Thessalonian Christians like *Paul only cares about your money*, or *He only cares about building up a group of followers. He's looking for position, respect, importance. He's simply using you for what he can get out of you.* As evidence of this, they are saying (as we have seen), *Look at him: he left and you haven't heard from him since.*

But what those people are saying about Paul is not true. He deeply loves the Thessalonian church, and he wishes that he could be with them. And so Paul takes time to express the intensity of his love, his affection, and his concern for them. He wants them to understand what his motivations really are in ministry.

I've wanted to come back, Paul is saying. *In fact, I've tried.* **Verse 17** explains that he has been "torn away ... in person not in heart." He has been thinking of them and praying for them. He "endeavoured the more eagerly and with great desire to see [them] face to face." He has been longing to see them. Over and over again he has tried to come back (**v 18**).

Paul will continue with this theme in **verses 19-20**. But first, it is worth pausing to consider the explanation he gives for why he did not return to Thessalonica.

A Pastor's Warning

Paul adds a warning, almost in passing. He says, "Satan hindered us" (**v 18**).

How exactly did Satan do that? The **commentators** have a number of interesting suggestions.

1. Some think that Paul was indicating that there was opposition to his ministry in Thessalonica, and this was what was keeping him from being able to come back to the Thessalonians. Some have suggested that the civil leaders in Thessalonica had actually put in place legal restrictions against Paul and his team barring them from coming back. As we've seen, the team had been at the center of a riot in Thessalonica (see Acts 17:1-9), and so maybe the civil leaders had actually passed a legal prohibition on Paul's return.

2. Another reason why Paul may not have been able to come back could be because of sin and scandal in the church in Corinth, which he had to deal with even from Athens.

3. It's also a possibility that Paul's mysterious "thorn in the flesh" (2 Corinthians 12:7) kept him from being able to come back to them. For 2,000 years, commentators have speculated on what that thorn in the flesh was. It's possible it was a physical malady. But we don't know. What we do know is that, in that same verse in 2 Corinthians, Paul also calls it "a messenger of Satan."

In the end, we don't know exactly how it was that Satan hindered Paul from returning to Thessalonica. But Paul does seem to be sure that Satan is behind his inability to get back to the Thessalonians. He doesn't drop the idea: later, in 1 Thessalonians 3:5, he tells us that one of his worries while he has been away from the Thessalonians is that the tempter may have come and tempted them. That is, Paul is concerned that a real, personal evil is not only opposing his ability to come back and minister to the Thessalonians but may be attempting to undermine the Thessalonians themselves in their faith.

This has huge implications. In this world, we not only have to deal with the allurement of the world toward sin or with the enticement to sin that comes from the flesh, our own inclinations. We also have to deal with the devil. There is a being in this world, older than humanity, who has a design to destroy you forever. The apostle Paul believed that with all his heart, and so he writes about it here.

It is worth asking yourself: do *I* believe this? I do. I've seen the devil at work. When people who know better look me in the eye and act against their own best interest—both their best interest here and their best interest hereafter—I smell that demon from the **pit**. Elsewhere, Paul calls him "the evil one" (2 Thessalonians 3:3) and "the tempter" (1 Thessalonians 3:5). There is a real evil being in this world who wants to test you—to sift you like wheat. We need to factor that into our thinking.

This is not an excuse to say, "The devil made me do it. I don't have any personal responsibility." The Bible never absolves us of our personal responsibility by appeal to Satan. We always have to look at our own hearts. We always have to consider the total context of sin in our lives, which we are each responsible for. But we must also remember that there is a person that wants to destroy us: Satan, the devil. And we cannot fight him on our own.

In his great hymn, "A Mighty Fortress Is Our God," which is a paraphrase of Psalm 46, Martin Luther wrote:

For still our ancient foe
Doth seek to work us woe;
His craft and power are great,
And, armed with cruel hate,
On earth is not his equal.

Luther believed in the reality of Satan, just as Paul did, and he knew that we do not by nature have the power within us to withstand him. That is why he says, "On earth is not his equal." But, later on in the hymn, Luther says that there *is* someone more than equal to Satan's power—someone who is, in fact, far greater than Satan:

Did we in our own strength confide,
Our striving would be losing;
Were not the right Man on our side,
The Man of God's own choosing.

We have "the right Man on our side": we have the Lord Jesus Christ, who died to liberate us from the bondage and power of sin and Satan. Not only this but also...

That word above all earthly powers,
No thanks to them, abideth;
The Spirit and the gifts are ours
Through Him who with us sideth.

We have the Spirit and his gifts. We have the third Person of the Trinity indwelling us, uniting us to Christ, and gifting us with all we need to live the Christian life.

Flesh and blood will not prevail against the devil. It is vitally important to remember that in our marriages, in our families, in our churches, and in our workplaces. The devil wants to destroy us by tempting us to respond sinfully in any and every difficult relationship or situation. How do we fight him? Through knowing the Man who is on our side and by relying on his Spirit and his gifts. The apostle John wrote, "The reason the Son of God appeared was to destroy the works of the devil" (1 John 3:8). This destruction was achieved at the cross and is taking place even now as the Spirit works in believers to God's glory. John wrote those words to people who "have overcome the evil one" (2:14). How have they done so? Because "the word of God abides in you."

Paul is so kind, even in the midst of reminding the Thessalonian Christians that he loves them, as to remind them that Satan sought to hinder him and to tempt them. Satan works to hinder, to oppose, to accuse, and to tempt us. We must rely on spiritual weapons to respond. We can trust that the Lord Jesus has been, is being, and will be victorious.

A Pastor's Hope and Glory

If we have seen nothing else so far in this letter, we have seen that Paul's life was not easy or comfortable. So imagine that a believer walked up to Paul toward the end of his life and said, *Paul, you've been beaten, you've been left for dead, you've been shipwrecked, you've been stranded, you've been slandered, you've been falsely accused, you've been put in chains. What's in it for you? Why do you do this?*

Paul's answer might well have been 1 Thessalonians **2:19-20**: "For what is our hope or joy or crown of boasting before our Lord Jesus at his coming? Is it not you? For you are our glory and joy."

Remember, there were people in Thessalonica who were saying, *Paul's in it for money. Paul's in it for ambition. Paul's in it for praise and fame.* But Paul says, *You want to know what I'm in it for? I'm in it for you.*

He pictures a scene. The Lord Jesus Christ has come, and Paul is before him. What is his boast before the Lord? What reward is he going to get from the Lord? Paul says, *You, before the Lord Jesus. You, with the Lord Jesus. You, safe home with the Lord Jesus on the day of his return.* The Thessalonians themselves—along with countless others with whom he has shared the gospel and in whom he has seen the Lord at work—are Paul's joy and crown. They are what he boasts about. That's what makes him do this. That's what makes him work night and day. That's what enables him to bear the anxiety and the pressure and the persecution. He is looking forward to that day when his Christian brothers are safe home with Jesus at his return. That's his reward.

In a previous life I was a youth director in a church, and one of the great fears and terrors that I had was that I would go off on a trip with 50 kids and come back with 49. Whether we went to massive amusement parks, big cities, beach retreats, or foreign mission trips, I always spent the whole time we were away thinking, "Lord, just get me back with all 50 of those kids." And when at last we pulled into the parking lot of the church and all of them were distributed to their parents and were happily on the way home, I always felt that I must be the most relieved human being on the planet.

That's the kind of scene the apostle Paul is pushing us to imagine here. He is saying, *You want to know what I'm in it for? I'm in it for the day when I hand you over to Jesus and you're safe home for eternity.*

Paul spent his life making sure that people like the Thessalonians were happy and safe—not temporarily happy and safe but everlastingly. And that meant he had to fight when they were tempted to swap their eternal happiness for cheap, temporary happiness. He had to fight their sin. He had to fight the world. He had to fight the flesh. He had to fight the devil. And those things did not leave Paul without scars. But he did it all because he wanted to be there on the day when they were safe home with the Lord Jesus Christ. He knew he would be able to say, *There they are, Jesus. They're safe with you now. That's all the reward I want. I just want them safe home.*

> Paul spent his life making sure that people were happy and safe— everlastingly.

Who do you know who is like Paul, ready to pour their lives out for others just to get them there? These people are ready to put blinkers on us so we won't be pulled off the pathway. Their message is always "Keep going. Keep going. Look to the finish line"—because they want us to be there on that day when Jesus returns. That's what Paul's saying to the Thessalonians. That's my hope. That's my crown. That's my glory. That's my joy—to get you safe home with Jesus. And for whom are *you* going to be like Paul?

This is what it looks like to live life in the light of Jesus' return. It's not only to fight temptation ourselves because we know that we're looking forward to something greater. It's not only to seek the help of the righteous Man, who can defeat the devil, and of his Spirit, who dwells within us. It's also to give ourselves to helping others in the fight—praying for, teaching, supporting, encouraging, and rebuking our brothers and sisters in the faith, filled with the joyful hope that one day we will see them before Jesus, being welcomed home.

Questions for reflection

1. Why is it a problem not to take the devil seriously? How does it help to remember that Jesus is stronger?

2. In what areas do you need to grow in love for your fellow Christians? What will you pray for God's help with?

3. Who are you looking after in the faith? Who could you describe as your glory and joy—someone you are longing to see safe home with Jesus? How can you invest in those people this week? Or if there is no one, who could you invest in?

5. THE GOAL OF MINISTRY

Chapter 3 of 1 Thessalonians is a continuation of Paul's thought at the end of chapter 2. After he had tried and tried to come back to the Thessalonians and couldn't, finally he sent Timothy to be with them. In **3:1-5**, he expresses how both Timothy's ministry among them and Paul's own ministry before that were designed to prepare the Thessalonian church to suffer trials and afflictions. Then **verses 6-8** describe both what news Timothy had brought back to Paul and how Paul responded to it.

The Purpose of Ministry

Paul could not come to the Thessalonians himself, and so he sent Timothy, "our brother and God's coworker in the gospel of Christ" (**v 1**)—even though this meant that Paul would be left alone in Athens. Timothy was sent "to establish and exhort you in your faith" (**v 2**). Paul wanted the Thessalonian Christians, first, to be rooted and grounded in the faith, and second, to be encouraged in that faith. And so he sent Timothy for ministry.

That's what good pastors want their ministry to result in: the members of their congregation being strengthened, grounded, and established in the truth and encouraged, exhorted, and comforted in their faith. (And the same goes for small-group leaders, youth leaders, and anyone in any form of church ministry.) Why is that the goal? "That no one be moved by these afflictions" (**v 3**).

Paul wants to prepare the Thessalonian church for suffering. He wants them to stand fast even though they know that Paul is experiencing afflictions—which they will too, "for you yourselves know that we are destined for this" (**v 3**). Paul elaborates on this in **verse 4**: "When we were with you, we kept telling you beforehand that we were to suffer affliction, just as it has come to pass, and just as you know."

Suffering, affliction, and **trials** in the Christian life should not be a surprise. We are destined for them. They are certain to come. It is not that they *may* come or that they *might* come or that they *could* come. Paul says they are *destined* to come.

How can we be prepared for them? By being rooted and grounded, by being exhorted and encouraged, by being established and strengthened in the truth and in our faith. That's how a pastor prepares his church to endure whatever trials or afflictions are coming. That is also how we can each prepare one another.

A few years ago Matt Chandler, the pastor of The Village Church in Fort Worth, Texas, became convinced that part of his job as pastor was to prepare his congregation to suffer. He wanted to make them into a church that could suffer joyfully—being honest about their struggles but finding hope and help in the Lord. It turned out that he, in preparing them to suffer well and to respond to the afflictions of life in a faithful way, was preparing himself to suffer too.

One of the first things that happened was that he was diagnosed with a brain tumor (from which he since appears to have been miraculously healed). Since then there have been numerous trials that have proved the importance of him working to prepare his people—as well as himself—to suffer well together (see Matt's book *Joy in the Sorrow*). We all need this preparation, so that when the inevitable suffering comes, we are not "moved" (**v 3**)—that is, we are not defeated by it. Instead we are able, although perhaps through tears, to say:

Though great distress my soul befell,
The Lord my God did all things well.

("All Praise to God, Who Reigns Above,"
Johann J. Shütz and Frances E. Cox).

Paul wants us to come through affliction and suffering by faith in Christ. When we are established and strengthened in faith, in the truth, and in the gospel, we can resist Satan as he opposes, accuses, and tempts us. We can withstand trials and tribulations and afflictions—not being defeated by them because we know by faith that God intends them for our eternal good.

Timothy's Good News

It is clear from 2:17 all the way to **3:4** how worried Paul is about the Thessalonians. He has expressed in strong terms how much he wanted to see them and minister to them. Now in **verse 5** we learn why he is so concerned: "I sent to learn about your faith, for fear that somehow the tempter had tempted you and our labor would be in vain."

He's worried that the slanderers are getting to them. He's worried that the persecution is knocking them off track. He's worried that they may be wavering in the faith. He's anxious to be with them so that he can encourage them.

> This is extravagant language that Paul is choosing.

But in **verse 6** it's almost like Timothy suddenly came through the door as Paul was writing, and said, *Paul, good news! They're all trusting in Christ. They're standing firm in the word. They're walking in the faith.* There's a gigantic sigh of relief in **verse 6**—you can still hear it across 2,000 years: "But now that Timothy has come to us from you, and has brought us the good news of your faith and love..."

Timothy has reported to Paul that the Thessalonians are doing well spiritually, are continuing with the Lord, and are established in faith and love, and Paul calls this "good news." That is a common phrase today, but Paul is using a specific word here which usually refers to the gospel message. This is actually the only time that Paul calls anything that is not the announcement of the gospel of Jesus Christ "good news." So this is extravagant language that he is choosing to use. He was so concerned about the Thessalonians that when he hears the report he says, in effect, *Timothy brought me gospel*. He is not saying that Timothy preached him a good gospel sermon; he is saying that Timothy gave a good spiritual report about the Thessalonians. This expresses how wonderful that news is.

Notice that Paul's relief is not because they're not going through hard times. It's because they are standing firm in Christ and growing in "faith and love" (**v 6**), even in the midst of afflictions. This should challenge us. What do we dream of for our lives? What do parents dream of for their children? What is the best news we could hear for ourselves or about them? To marry a nice person and be a good husband or wife? To have a nice life, with no major illnesses or big problems? To have a good job and be respected in the community? All of those things are good things. But far more important than any of those is that we and our loved ones remain standing firm in Christ and growing in faith and love.

After a church service some years ago, a young man came and met me at the door. He had been married for ten years. Three years into his marriage, it had been hanging by a thread; but God turned it all around by bringing him and his wife to faith in Christ and then into a Bible-believing church, where they heard the gospel preached every week and the Bible faithfully taught. They began to work through the issues in their marriage. Then they had a child who was diagnosed with autism.

No parent would say, "I hope my son will struggle in his marriage and have a child with autism." But through all his difficult circumstances, that young man was growing in faith and love. When I met him, he was preaching the gospel at a rescue mission in downtown Birmingham, Alabama every week. He wanted to be involved in the work of God's kingdom. He was standing firm in the faith.

Is this what we pray for one another, and for our sons and daughters: that they'd stand firm in Christ and that they'd grow in faith and love, and not just that circumstances would be easy? Of course it is natural to want circumstances to be the best for those we love; but above all, we should desire that no matter what the circumstances are, they may stand firm in Christ and grow in faith and love.

I love what the 16th-century **Reformer**, John Calvin, says about faith and love: "In these two words [Paul] comprehends briefly the entire sum of true piety" (*Commentaries on the Epistle of Paul to the Philippians, Colossians, and Thessalonians*, translated by John Pringle, on 1 Thessalonians 3:6). That is, all godliness can be summed up in faith and love. Believing God's promises and his word, trusting in Jesus as he is offered in the gospel—that is faith. Loving God, loving one another, loving our neighbors—that is love.

If "faith and love" sums up the whole of the Christian life, then Timothy's report is that the Thessalonians are living the Christian life. They're believing God's promises; they're believing his word; they're trusting in Christ as he's offered in the gospel. They're loving God; they're loving one another; they're loving their neighbor. That is what Paul's prayer has been for the Thessalonian Christians, and that is why he shows such relief.

Parental Pastoring

"In all our distress and affliction we have been comforted about you through your faith." (**v 7**)

It is wonderful how sometimes somebody else's faith encourages you. Have you ever had a Christian friend who is going through an incredibly hard time—a situation that makes you think, "I'm not sure how I would handle that"—and then you have watched as that friend continues trusting in the Lord, believing God's promises, not becoming bitter but remaining absolutely determined that they will reach the light at the end of the tunnel? Seeing that kind of faith is so encouraging. That is what Paul says has "comforted" him as he's heard about the Thessalonians in the midst of his own trials.

But Paul is saying even more than that here. "Now we live, if you are standing fast in the Lord" (**v 8**). That "if" isn't meant to put any question mark on how the Thessalonians are doing. It is meant to emphasize that what makes Paul able to say, "Now we live" is the report that the Thessalonians are standing firm in the faith.

Now *that's* extravagant language. This isn't just relief—a pastor saying, "I feel like my ministry's not a failure now because you're doing well in the Lord." There's no indication in this verse that Paul was worried about the success of his ministry. It's not about him and how he feels about himself.

This is the kind of language people use when they fall in love. They write to each other saying things like "You make me live," or "I'm alive for the first time." It's not just relief or confidence in yourself; it's a deep, deep thrill. Paul loves the Thessalonian Christians that much. Paul has a love for these Christians like a father and a mother have for their children. His reaction is not *Thank heavens, I'm not a failure because you're doing well*. It is the reaction of a parent: *My children are doing well in the Lord. My children are standing firm in the faith. Thank God, I rejoice. My heart is filled with thanksgiving to the Lord.*

The pastor and author Tim Keller once said to me, "When you're a parent, you are never more happy than your least happy child." That is how much parents care about the children's happiness and their well-being. If you have four kids and three of them are doing well in their faith but one of them is not, it weighs on you. You think about it all the time because you want each one of them to be happy—eternally happy. So when they come through those trying times you say, "Yes, I can live again. My children are standing firm in Christ. They're growing in faith and love."

That's the kind of emotional investment that Paul is expressing here. *I was dying inside when I thought that you weren't doing well. Now I can live again.* The Thessalonian Christians are Paul's beloved children in the Lord. And so he's relieved, he's thankful, he's joyful, and he's overwhelmed at the good news that the Thessalonians are displaying faith and love. He has invested his heart in them and their ongoing walk with Christ—he has risked having his heart broken because he loves them. When it comes to our own church families and those the Lord has given us to walk alongside, we are to do the same.

Questions for reflection

1. Why are Paul's words in verses 3-4 helpful as we face difficulties in life? What do you think it could look like to prepare ourselves for affliction?

2. What do you hope for in your life and/or in your children's lives (including spiritual children)? How does what you've read in this chapter challenge you on what your greatest hopes should be?

3. What is one thing you can do to be more like Paul in this passage?

PART TWO

Paul is joyful and thankful because he has heard that the Thessalonian Christians are standing firm in their faith. Now in **verses 9-13**, Paul first tells the Thessalonians again how thankful he is for them and then explains what he's praying for them. These verses, too, are marked by rejoicing.

Fitting Superlatives

One of the things that my family enjoyed most about conversations with my dad while he was alive was the number of **superlatives** that he would use. These were often associated with good food. If we were at a seafood restaurant, we were likely to hear these words: "I believe that that was the best crab soup I have ever had in my entire life!" Or if we had just had a delicious steak, we were likely to hear "I don't believe I have ever put a better piece of meat in my mouth!" Or if we were at a barbecue place, he might say, "You know, I don't believe I have ever had better hash in my entire life!" We loved hearing his superlatives every time we had a good meal. These were not empty phrases—they were his way of expressing just how much he had enjoyed his food.

That is the kind of tone Paul is using here in **verse 9** as he writes, "What thanksgiving can we return to God for you, for all the joy that we feel for your sake before our God … ?" He is so grateful and so joyful that he can't possibly express enough thanks to God. It's as if words just aren't enough.

This type of writing continues in **verse 10**. After giving thanks for the Thessalonians' faith and love, Paul goes on to say, "We pray most earnestly night and day." Paul could not pray any more earnestly than he was doing, and he could not pray any more often than he was doing.

What is he praying so much for? "That we may see you face to face and supply what is lacking in your faith."

Paul had only been able to be with them and teach them for a few weeks, and then he had had to leave the city. Now he wants to come back to supply what is lacking in their faith. How is he going to do that? He can't create faith in them himself; he can't grow their faith himself. Only the Holy Spirit can do that. What Paul means to do is to teach them the word of God. That is the truth that supplies what is lacking in our faith. Paul wants to instruct them in the gospel so that their faith will grow. As he puts it in Romans 10:17, "Faith comes from hearing, and hearing through the word of Christ." So when Paul says he wants to come and supply what is lacking in the Thessalonians' faith, what he is saying is that he wants their faith to be grown by truth—the truth of the word. And this teaching is going to be designed to grow them in love.

We see this clearly in 1 Timothy 1:5. Paul has received a charge from Jesus to take up a gospel ministry—a ministry which he has passed on to Timothy. And he says to Timothy, "The aim of our charge is love that issues from a pure heart and a good conscience and a sincere faith." Paul wants Christians to love God, to love one another, and to love their neighbors with a sincere, blameless love. That is his aim in ministry and his goal in his teaching and instruction: that there would be disciples who love.

If we don't understand that this is how truth functions, we'll miss the whole point of why we gather **Lord's Day** after Lord's Day, why we study the Bible during the week, and why we have seminaries and schools that teach the word of God. God is not in the business of simple information transfer, which has no relevance to real life. He's not trying to cram your mind full of little facts so that you know more than the people around you but still act the same way you always did. I often say to seminary students, "You can learn about the **hypostatic union** of the natures of Jesus Christ and still go home and be a jerk to your wife." If they do that, they are missing the point. That is not what God's truth is designed for.

Everything that God says in his word is designed to change how we live in relation to him and in relation to one another. God's truth is designed to transform your life. That is why in Romans 12:2 Paul says, "Be transformed by the renewal of your mind, that by testing you may discern what is the will of God, what is good and acceptable and perfect." It is our minds that are first of all renewed and transformed, with the result that our behavior comes into line with what God wants and loves. And it is by God's word that we learn what God's will is and how that looks in every area of our individual lives. That's what Paul is saying here: that we grow in faith and in love by hearing and receiving the truth.

Paul felt that the Thessalonians needed him to visit them in order to supply what was lacking in their faith. He was an apostle, specifically equipped by God to explain the truth. For us today, the Bible is what supplies the truth to us; it's there that we find the apostolic record of the life of Jesus and the apostolic teaching for the people of Jesus. 2 Peter 1:3 tells us that God's "divine power has granted to us all things that pertain to life and godliness, through the knowledge of him who called us." In the Scriptures we have all the knowledge we need to grow in faith and love.

Love Leads to Godliness

If the result of being grounded in God's word is to grow in love, Paul next tells us that the result of growing in love is that we can be established in **holiness**.

This is very interesting. Paul starts by turning what he has said about longing to see the Thessalonians into a prayer: "May our God and Father himself, and our Lord Jesus, direct our way to you" (1 Thessalonians **3:11**). Then in **verses 12-13** he continues, "May the Lord make you increase and abound in love for one another and for all … so that he may establish your hearts blameless in holiness." Paul is saying that it is impossible for us to grow in holiness outside of the context of loving relationships with one another as Christians and a loving attitude toward all people.

In other words, Christian godliness is not just a matter of you sitting down on your own and saying, "I'm going to cultivate this particular virtue in my life." Let's say that I look through the list of the **fruit of the Spirit** in Galatians 5:22-23, and I decide I'm going to be a more faithful person. I'll soon find I can't do that by myself. There has to be somebody else around before I can be more faithful. Faithfulness can't exist with only one person—it has to be faithfulness *to* somebody. Or let's say I decide I'm going to be kinder. Again, I have to have somebody else around if I'm going to be kind.

Other people also help us to grow in godliness in the sense that they can keep us accountable. Sometimes we struggle to see our own faults, and we

> The virtues of the Christian life cannot be cultivated in isolation.

need others to point them out to us. And, conversely, we benefit from the encouragement of someone saying, "I know you've been trying to become more patient (or peaceful or faithful or kind), and I thought you handled that situation really well. Praise God for his work in you." When we love each other and seek to help each other grow in love, that's when we increase and abound in love as a community.

The point is this: the virtues of the Christian life cannot be cultivated in isolation from other Christians. We need to be in community, and we need to be accountable to one another, in order to cultivate the virtues of the Christian life.

You might say there are some virtues on that list in Galatians 5 which don't require another person. Joy or peace, for example: aren't those just feelings you can have on your own? It's true that you can feel joyful or peaceful when you're just sitting alone, perhaps when you are enjoying God's word or speaking to him in prayer or simply feeling thankful for what he has given you. But the real challenge comes when other people are around—people who are difficult or hostile or demanding. Anyone can feel peaceful when they're on vacation or in their favorite places and able to do exactly what they like. But you really know the Spirit is at work when you have the kind of joy and peace that Paul wrote about: joy in the midst of suffering (Philippians 1:17-18; 4:11-13), a pursuit of peace with others—including those who are not easy to live in peace with—wherever possible (Romans 12:18), and an experience of the peace that surpasses understanding (Philippians 4:7).

Since we become established in godliness when are with "one another," we're going to have to learn to forgive one another and bear with one another. Love is often going to have to cover a multitude of sins. Love is going to have to think the best of others when we're tempted to think the worst. Love is going to have to be willing to put up with people who are difficult to be with or who are just different than us—and not just put up with them but welcome them like a brother or sister. All of that is going to be necessary to our growing in godliness.

Godliness is the thing that makes the world look at the church and say, "They're not like us." If we're not godly—if we behave and think in the same ways the world does—then people will say, "You don't have anything to teach us." But when our priorities are different, when our behavior is different, and when our aspirations are different, the world says, "Well, they're a little weird, but they might have something I need to listen to." And godliness, which witnesses to the world that the Holy Spirit is at work in us, won't manifest itself if we are not increasing and abounding in love. That is the starting point for all the other Christian virtues. Increase in love is necessary for establishment in godliness. That's what Paul is saying here.

It's a glorious passage, and it sets before us some big aspirations. Paul uses another superlative. We are not just to "increase" but also to "abound" in love (1 Thessalonians **3:12**)—to be filled up with love, be overflowing with love, and be noticeable for the amount of love we are able to give.

Do you want to grow in faith and love? Do you want to grow in the truth? Do you desire to be more godly as a result of your growth?

When you desire these things—and even if you don't yet desire them—you must realize that what is required is to deliberately commit yourself and ask the Holy Spirit to make you increase and abound in love. He is the one who will work in you and who will work through the word to transform you; but you need to commit yourself to his will and to doing what God's word says.

Blameless at His Coming

Paul ends his prayer for the Thessalonian Christians in **verse 13** by reminding them of the coming of our Lord Jesus. He prays "that [God] may establish your hearts blameless in holiness before our God and Father, at the coming of our Lord Jesus with all his **saints**."

How do you live life in light of Jesus' return? You long for godliness, you pursue love, and you grow in faith and in love.

Love is going to mean thinking about other people before yourself. It's going to be about seeking their best interest before your own. It's going to entail overlooking offenses and growing in patience and forbearance toward those who upset you. It's going to involve faithfully sticking by people even when they are at their most difficult. It's going to mean being generous with your time and money and possessions.

That is how you stand fast in Christ. Faith and love should go together. Don't you love that combination? You may look out in the church and see people that are strong in love and weak in faith, or strong in faith and weak in love. But here Paul is saying, *No, those things should go together.* A strong faith, grounded and established in the truth, leads to hearts that love God and love others. Both are necessary to live in light of the day when Jesus returns.

Questions for reflection

1. How can our Bible-reading help us to grow in faith and love?

2. Why do we need others to help us grow in holiness?

3. In what way do you long to "increase and abound" in love? What will you pray for yourself and for your church community as a result of reading this passage?

6. HOW TO PLEASE GOD

At this point we are only halfway through the letter; we have two full chapters to go. Why is Paul saying, "Finally" (1 Thessalonians 4:1)?! It is because we are now getting to the point of the letter. All the way through the first three chapters, Paul has been speaking about the Thessalonians' faith and reminding them of his past ministry among them. Now, "finally," he is getting to the instructions that he wants to give them.

Paul does this regularly in his letters. Ephesians 1 – 3 is full of wonderful theology, and then suddenly in chapter 4 you start getting teaching about living the Christian life. The same thing happens in Romans. It's primarily **theology** and doctrine in chapters 1 – 11; then suddenly in 12:1 we read, "I appeal to you therefore, brothers, by the mercies of God [which Paul has been enumerating throughout chapters 1 – 11], to present your bodies as a living sacrifice…" Then chapters 12 – 14 are filled with exhortations about Christian living. So, this is a regular pattern for Paul: doctrine, then duty; faith, then practice; truth, then life. For Paul, all truth serves to inform Christian living. It teaches us how we are to live.

In 1 Thessalonians 4 – 5, Paul will address the issue of sexual immorality; he will discuss vocation and how we go about our work; and he will also address the issue of death and our response to the death of our loved ones. Sex, work, and death—these are perennial issues, important in every culture and in every generation. Paul is going to give specific commands about how we are to live life in light of Jesus' return in those areas.

4:1-2 is Paul's introduction to this section. Here, Paul gives a framework that will, if you understand it, change the way you view obedience in the Christian life. It will have a dramatic effect on the way that you look at God's commandments and the way that you view obedience and duty toward him. It will give you a joy and a delight in those things. So it is worth paying close attention.

It's Good to Be Pushed

"Brothers, we ask and urge you in the Lord Jesus…" (**v 1**). The word "urge" is an important one. It helps us to understand what Paul is doing here and why. He has taught the Thessalonian Christians a robust theology of grace. They are saved by what Jesus has done for them, not by what they do. But that does not prevent him from urging them to do things. This is because the apostle Paul is like a personal trainer, pushing Christians in order to help them to achieve their goal. He is not simply telling them off or giving them a list of dry instructions. He is urging them on.

Let's say you have gotten a little flabby around the middle. You decide you need to do something about this: you'll go to a personal trainer who will help you get the weight off. You want someone who's on your side—someone who will urge you to accomplish what you've set out to do. It will not bother you when your personal trainer pushes you because you want to achieve your goal and you know that being pushed will help you.

> Paul is like a personal trainer, urging them on.

It is a similar situation for the Thessalonian Christians. They know that they are saved by grace, and not by trying hard or doing well or being nice or being better. They trust in Jesus. But they also know that one of the reasons that God has saved them is so that they will be conformed to the image of his Son (Romans 8:29). So they want to be more like their Savior. And therefore, when Paul urges them to pursue that very thing, they know he is urging them as their friend in order to get them to where God wants them to go.

We should not be surprised to see Paul urging and imploring and commanding and directing. He is not forgetting what he has taught about God's grace, which alone can save. Rather, he is practicing a very important principle: that grace reigns through righteousness (Romans 5:21). That is, God's grace shows itself to have had an impact on us through our growing Christian maturity. Therefore, Paul urges us to behave as increasingly mature Christians.

How to Please God

The rest of 1 Thessalonians **4:1** summarizes the purpose of the commands which the remaining two chapters of the letter will contain. It is all about "how you ought to walk and to please God."

"Walk" is one of several metaphors used in the New Testament to describe the Christian life. It implies slow, unspectacular, but steady progress. It is about how to live day by day as Christians. In the short time Paul was able to be with the Thessalonians, they had received teaching from him on how to live the Christian life.

And fundamentally, that included how "to please God." This is a phrase that is really important and very easily misunderstood. Many of us have experienced relationships in which, no matter what we do to try to please somebody, it's never enough; there's no extra effort that we could make that isn't going to be either overlooked or criticized. So we end up feeling like a hamster on a wheel: we are working really, really hard to try to please the other person, but we are never quite succeeding.

It would be easy to read that we are to live to "please God" and think of him like that: hard to please and always demanding more. But that's not what Paul is talking about. He does not mean that the believer has to please God in the sense that what we do becomes the reason that he loves us. No—God already loves us. If we are in Christ, he loves us as his beloved children. So pleasing God is more similar to a child pleasing their father. I loved to please my father. It killed me to disappoint him—not because he was difficult to please but because I knew and loved what it felt like to experience his pleasure. There was nothing like the affection and affirmation that I received from him. There is a huge thrill in pleasing a person whom you love and who is predisposed to be pleased by what you do because they love you.

This is the kind of relationship Jesus has with his Father. When Jesus was baptized, the Father's voice came from heaven, saying, "This is my beloved Son, with whom I am well pleased" (Matthew 3:17). The Father was expressing his pleasure in his Son. It is no surprise that Jesus said that he loves to please his Father (John 8:29).

When we put our faith in Jesus, we are united to him and are treated by God as if we were his beloved Son. We are actually adopted into his own family (see, for example, Romans 8:14-19). Therefore, God, as our heavenly Father, is already pleased with us. And when he sees us seeking to love and serve people—seeking to do his will in this world—he takes even greater pleasure in that.

When we grasp this, we will love to please God, just as I loved to please my earthly father. Paul is urging the Thessalonians to live so that, like Jesus, their constant aspiration is to please the Lord—and to experience his pleasure in their pleasing him. They can view their obedience to God in light of the pleasure the Lord takes in them. When they get up in the morning, their attitude can (and ought to) be, "I want to please my heavenly Father, because there is nothing in this world like knowing that I am loved by him and knowing that in my conduct today I can bring pleasure to him."

The command to please God and to walk in his way is therefore not just a set of instructions. It is really an encouragement to please someone who is already disposed to be pleased. This becomes clearer in the second half of 1 Thessalonians **4:1**: Paul had told them how they could "please God, *just as you are doing*…" (my emphasis). Paul is not saying, *You dummies are doing it all wrong!* Rather, he is saying,

You're doing what you're supposed to be doing. Now, keep on doing it! "Do so more and more"!

Two Implications

This is important for a thousand reasons. Let me outline just two! First, this truth is significant for those who are involved in a relationship in which the other person can never be pleased. We will all be involved in such relationships in our lives at some time or other. If your goal in life is to get satisfaction out of that relationship by pleasing the other person, you will be deeply hurt. But if your goal is to please your heavenly Father, then you can do anything because you know that your Father *will* take pleasure in you—especially when he sees you loving and serving someone who is not going to love or serve you back. He'll say, *This is my child, who is like my Son, in whom I am well pleased.* You will be able to cope with people who can never be pleased because you will know that God is already disposed to be pleased by you.

Second, it is also significant for those of us who are approval junkies—what the **Puritans** used to call "man-pleasers." This describes people who get their sense of significance and security from others' estimation of them and are always looking for compliments—doing things for no other reason than to gain someone's affirmation. But this sets us up for disappointment and resentment (if no one notices us and our successes or good deeds) or brittle pride (if they do). This truth about how to please God will set you free from constantly craving human approval. When it is God whose approval we want—when his "well done" is the only one that we are looking for—that allows us to be freed from the shackles of what other people think. It stops us from endlessly getting up on our hamster wheels in an effort to please other people.

Our heavenly Father is the one we are to want to please more than anyone else in this world. And he delights and takes pleasure in what we do to please him. That means we can have fulfillment in every relationship and every season of life.

Paul means to encourage the Thessalonian Christians—and us—to keep going in love and good deeds.. Obedience in the Christian life is not a list of things to do "or else." It is a way of bringing God pleasure and feeling God's pleasure. What should we say as we read Paul's words here? "I can please the Lord if I do these things? Where do I sign up?"

Truth and Obedience

In 1 Thessalonians **4:2**, Paul gives his readers a reminder. "You know what instructions we gave you through the Lord Jesus." The "instructions" here refer back to the fact that "you received from us how you ought to walk" (**v 1**). In other words, Paul had already taught them about how they were to live. Now he's about to reiterate some of these instructions.

It's important to note that in **verse 1** Paul urged them "in the Lord Jesus"; now he says he has instructed them "through the Lord Jesus." In the Great Commission, when Jesus sent his disciples out, he said, "Make **disciples** ... teaching them to observe all that I have commanded you" (Matthew 28:19-20). We are not just to hear what he has commanded but also to obey it. Paul here is saying what Jesus has already said; his instructions for the Christian life stem from Jesus. And it is the truth about Jesus that must inform how Christians are to behave.

We'll get to the specific instructions in a moment—but this reminder is important and worth pausing over. All Christian teaching is connected to living. All truth is practical: it's meant to change the way we live. Paul is reminding the Thessalonian Christians that they were not taught the truth so that they could be smarter than the pagans but so that they could live the Christian life. That was what Jesus meant.

Questions for reflection

1. Do you ever feel like obedience to God is a dry duty? How does this passage encourage you?

2. How does this passage help us not to be "approval junkies"?

3. What is one area in which you are finding it hard to obey God? How will this passage help you to pray for your own heart?

PART TWO

If I had to choose one passage in the Bible to explain the concept of sanctification, it would be 1 Thessalonians **4:3-8**. Sanctification means growing in godliness: living to righteousness and dying to sin more and more. It is not something we do on our own. In these verses Paul emphasizes the will of God, the call of God, and the empowerment of God in sanctification.

Within this framework of talking about sanctification, Paul's big pastoral concern here is sexual purity. He was writing to a congregation that lived in a time and a culture of sexual immorality—not unlike our own time and culture. This is why Paul majored on sexual immorality. It wasn't that Paul was prudish or that sexual immorality is absolutely the most important issue there is. It was that the Thessalonian Christians needed the apostle to address this issue, just as we do.

Holiness Comes from God

We see Paul's great concern here right away: "This is the will of God, your sanctification" (**v 3**).

There are a lot of books written on the subject of discerning God's will. Young people especially are often trying to figure it out. "Lord, what did you put me here for? What do you want me to do for the rest of my life? Where do you want me to work? Who do you want me to marry? Where do you want me to live? What do you want me to do with the gifts and abilities that you've given to me?"

We don't always know what the specific will of God is for us in our lives in those terms. But I can tell you this, on the basis of this verse: the will of God for your life is that you grow in holiness. For every Christian, whoever you are—whether you are male or female, whether you are young or old, whether you live in Jackson, Mississippi or Jaipur, India—it is God's will for you to grow in holiness.

God's will, God's plan, God's purpose for every Christian is sanctification: growing in godliness. In fact, if I had to give a one-sentence

summary of this whole passage, it would be this: God's will for you is
to be godly.

In **verses 7-8** Paul explains this further. "God has not called us for
impurity, but in holiness" (**v 7**). God has not called us to live impure,
immoral lives. He has literally called us into holiness. Just as we are
called into Christ to be his disciples and to be in fellowship with him,
so we are called into holiness. The reason why God has called you out
of darkness and into his marvelous light is not just to be forgiven but
also to be sanctified.

Paul does not say that we were holy and were therefore called. If
we were saved by our own holiness, we would all be in trouble because none of us can be holy on our own. What he means is that in
being saved *by* the blood of the Lord Jesus Christ, we are saved *for* a
life of holiness—a life of growing godliness. God has called us to that
in our salvation.

Next, in **verse 8** Paul emphasizes that God has given us his Holy
Spirit. This has become the most common name that Christians use to
designate the third Person of the Trinity; but in the Old Testament, the
most common name for the Holy Spirit is simply the "Spirit of God."
Here, Paul calls the Spirit "the Holy Spirit" in order to draw attention
to one of the things that he does: he grows us in holiness. To disregard
our calling to holiness would be to disregard the Spirit—and therefore
to disregard God.

God's will is your holiness, God's call to you was into holiness, and
God's gift to you is his Spirit so that you can grow in holiness. Sanctification is something that God is at work in you to achieve.

Pursuing Holiness

Nevertheless, sanctification is also something that we are to pursue
ourselves. In **verses 4:3-6**, Paul shows this by immediately giving a
specific application, an example of what he means by sanctification:
"that you abstain from sexual immorality" (**v 3**).

These may be very uncomfortable words for us, because Paul's words are just as applicable to us today as they were to the Thessalonians. We live in a world where same-sex attraction is celebrated and increasingly legalized, sex outside marriage has become a societal norm, and the very definition of marriage has become murky. There is a clear biblical pattern for sexual morality: sex is designed to be within a committed and faithful lifelong marriage between one man and one woman. But in the face of societal pressures, even Christians are letting go of this view. And, of course, even if we hold to the biblical view in theory, we are still faced with enormous temptations in sexual matters. Sexual immorality is a major issue in our culture and our churches—just as it was in the Thessalonian culture. That is why Paul is putting it right in his crosshairs.

When Paul tells the Thessalonian Christians to abstain from sexual immorality in **verse 3**, he uses the word *porneia*, a general term that refers to all kinds of sexual immorality. In particular, he wants them to control their bodily appetites (**v 4**). Abstaining from sexual immorality means "that each one of you know how to control his own body in holiness and honor, not in the passion of lust like the Gentiles who do not know God." The instruction is simple: *I know that the culture around you does not abstain from it, but in the church we are going to abstain. We're going to be different from the world around us.* These Christians are called to control their bodily appetites, their lust, and their passions, even while the Gentiles cry, *Just do whatever you feel! Do whatever you like!*

This is particularly striking when we remember that the Thessalonians were a majority-Gentile congregation: they may have had a small core of Jewish people, but they were mostly Gentiles, ethnically speaking. (All non-Jews are Gentiles.) Yet Paul says to them that he does not want them to act like Gentiles. For Paul, the primary source of identity is no longer ethnic. You either believe in the Lord Jesus Christ or you do not. That latter category is how he uses the word "Gentiles" here— you could read it as "non-Christians." Though the Thessalonian Christians were ethnically Gentiles, that was no longer their primary identity because now they were in Christ. That's why Paul could tell them not to act in the way the culture around them acted.

Sexual morality is a matter of self-control. We are not to be ruled and mastered by our own bodily appetites. We don't get our marching orders for how to live with one another and relate to one another sexually from how we feel at a given moment. We don't get them from the world. We get them from God's word.

The Impact of Immorality

In **verse 6**, Paul tells the Thessalonians not to "transgress" in this matter. That word means to cross the line, to trespass: in other words, to break the law of God.

Why does God care so much about our sexual morals? It is important to realize, first of all, that sexual immorality is not only serious when it involves directly hurting another human being. It is always serious because it always harms our relationship with God.

In the Old Testament, the major metaphor for being unfaithful to God is adultery: when the Israelites go after other gods, they are said to be committing spiritual adultery (e.g. Ezekiel 23:4, 36-37). Part of the reason for that is that in many of these other religions, especially in the worship of the false Canaanite god Baal, actual prostitution and adultery were involved in the religious rituals. But a much deeper reason is the truth that sexual immorality and spiritual unfaithfulness are fundamentally connected. 1 Corinthians 6:16-17 explains this: "Do you not know that he who is joined to a prostitute becomes one body with her? For, as it is written, 'The two will become one flesh.' But he who is joined to the Lord becomes one spirit with him." Our bodies, just as much as our souls, are Christ's. If we are in Christ, we should honor him with our bodies rather than being pushed and pulled by passion and lust. Sexual immorality dishonors and disregards our relationship with Christ, and it affects our relationship with him just as much as adultery would affect our relationship with our spouse.

A young man fresh out of college once came to me to tell me that he was really struggling in his faith. I had known him when he was in high school, and he had been one of the most mature boys of his age, but now he wasn't sure he believed in the existence of God anymore. I asked him, "Are you sleeping with your girlfriend?" And at once he looked like a ghost. It turned out that, yes, he was. And there was a direct connection between his spiritual crisis and his sexual immorality.

It's easy for young people to think, "This is just the season of life when I can enjoy myself. I can spend a few years doing whatever I want. When I get out of college, I'll settle down and get more serious about Jesus and about being faithful to one person, and it will all be fine." But it doesn't work that way. We cannot ignore God in this area and think that it will not impact our faith.

Sexual immorality is also serious for other reasons, of course. If you act inappropriately, immorally, and without purity in sexual matters, you are not just transgressing against God—you are wronging your brother. (This term includes women in Christ.) This is the phrase Paul adds in 1 Thessalonians **4:6**—"that no one transgress and wrong his brother in this matter."

When we are immoral, we are sinning against our brothers and sisters in Christ.

You may think that adultery and watching pornography are the only types of sexual immorality that harm others—both involve unfaithfulness to a spouse, and the latter also supports a deeply exploitative industry. Actually, in any type of sexual immorality, we are robbing our spouse (present or future) of what should belong only to them, and (if we are being immoral with someone else) we are stealing from someone else's present or future spouse too. But although those kinds of harm must be taken very seriously, it is not the case that they are the only harm involved in sexual immorality. When we are immoral, we are sinning against our brothers and sisters in

Christ (including those who will never get married) in any and every instance.

We have already seen Paul say to the Thessalonian Christians that sexual morality is important to mark the identity of the church—they are to act like Christians, not like the Gentiles (**v 5**). One of the ways in which we can show that the gospel is true and that the Holy Spirit is real and working in us is through the lives we live: lives that are distinguishable from the world around us. The Thessalonian Christians are called not to live like the pagans live, and that is going to be seen clearly in their fidelity to their spouses and in their sexual purity. A life of sexual immorality puts in peril our witness to the gospel.

Moreover, purity in sexual matters is absolutely essential for harmony in the congregation. Do adultery and other sexual sins lead to unity? Of course not. They always break it up. People take sides and form entrenched opinions about who is in the right. People decide that the leaders of the church should have done this or should have done that. Sexual immorality always fragments the unity of a congregation.

These are just some of the reasons why Christians should care about sexual purity. We do not care because we are repressed or because we are prudes but because we love God and we love people. We care about the witness of the church, and we care about the everlasting souls of the people we know.

A Solemn Warning

There are so many earthly ramifications of sexual impurity: marriages breaking up, families being torn apart, and lives being wounded and ruined. These things are dramatic and truly heartbreaking. And yet it is eternal concerns that are the most important, and these are what Paul focuses on here.

Why is it that we shouldn't transgress and wrong our brother? In the second half of **verse 6**, Paul says it is "because the Lord is an avenger in all these things." In **verse 8**, as we've already seen, he adds that "whoever disregards this, disregards not man but God, who gives his Holy Spirit to you." Paul is warning here that those who are sexually immoral—if they do not repent—will one day face God's avenging justice and wrath. Sexual impurity is disregarding God's call to holiness, which is disregarding God himself. That deservedly brings his anger.

This does not mean that sexual sin cannot be forgiven. In 1 Corinthians 6:11, after listing all manner of sexual immorality, Paul writes, "And such were some of you. But you were washed, you were sanctified, you were justified in the name of the Lord Jesus Christ." It is entirely possible to repent of these sins and be gloriously and graciously accepted by God.

Nor does this mean that true believers will never struggle with these things. The man who wrote more psalms than anyone else was an adulterer—**King David** (see 2 Samuel 11; Psalm 51). But a Christian must never make peace with these sins or seek to justify them. Whenever we have succumbed to temptation in these sins, our souls are in danger. That is why Paul gives us this solemn warning. He is saying that unrepentant sexually immoral people face the avenging justice and wrath of God. This is because, if God has called us to live in holiness, then to live in sexual immorality constitutes a rejection of that call. It simply makes no sense to say, "Jesus, I want to be your disciple, but I don't want to live the way you've called me to live." But those who attempt to justify their sexual immorality—whether it's watching pornography, acting upon same-sex attraction, or having sex outside marriage—are doing exactly that.

If you have given in to the temptation to live in sexual immorality of any kind, then you need to repent of those sins—and remember that the blood of Christ is sufficient to cover every sin of every one of his people. Fortunately, you are given an ally in your fight against temptation—the greatest ally of all. This is a spiritual battle and it must be fought in dependence upon the Holy Spirit. He is the one who sanctifies us. This is the will of God, "for God has not called us for impurity, but in holiness" (1 Thessalonians **4:7**).

Questions for reflection

1. Are you seeking God's will for a specific situation at the moment (or do you know anyone who is)? How does verse 3a help you?

2. What does the culture around you say about sexual conduct? What is the biggest temptation for you personally to conform with the culture?

3. Why is it so important to pursue holiness? What's the implication if we disregard holiness?

7. WE URGE YOU

Paul writes two important exhortations in 1 Thessalonians **4:9-12** about what it means to live life in light of Jesus' return. But before he gives those exhortations, he grounds these believers in an encouragement.

God-Taught

In **verse 9**, Paul says, "Now concerning brotherly love you have no need for anyone to write to you, for you yourselves have been taught by God to love one another." What an encouragement: to say that, in a way, they really don't need anyone to teach them about brotherly love because they're already showing it. Paul says a similar thing again in the first part of **verse 10**: "That indeed is what you are doing to all the brothers throughout Macedonia." He is complimenting them on the good job that they're doing of showing Christian love to visiting believers from other cities as well as within their own congregation.

But **verse 9** doesn't just show us what a great job the Thessalonian Christians are doing. It also teaches us that when we love fellow believers the way Jesus does, we are showing that we have been taught by God. This is an encouragement to us for two reasons.

First, Paul can see that God is at work in the hearts of the Thessalonians. We saw in chapter 4 of this book the importance of looking out for evidence of grace in one another, in order to keep ourselves from grumbling. Here is another reason to do so: because when we see such evidence, we can encourage one another about God's work in our lives. We need to have that kind of an eye as we look at the lives of our brothers and sisters—looking out for how grace is at work in their lives and then encouraging them by pointing it out. If we do not, both they and we are missing out on a great blessing.

Paul has that kind of eye, and so he can tell that God is at work in the Thessalonians' hearts. The kind of brotherly love they are showing can only come from the Holy Spirit. And therefore he tells them about it—not just to thank them for being nice but to remind them that God really is at work in them. It is a way of giving thanks for the evidence of the truth of Philippians 2:13—"It is God who works in you, both to will and to work for his good pleasure"—made manifest in their conduct.

Second, by saying that the Thessalonians are taught by God, Paul is acknowledging that the promises of God to his people have come to pass among the Thessalonians. In the original Greek language, the phrase "taught by God" is actually one word. Paul took the word "God" (*theos*) and the word "taught" (*didaktos*) and stuck them together—to make *theodidaktoi,* meaning "God-taught." Scholars think he invented this word because they cannot find any examples of it in Greek writing before Paul wrote this letter, and only a few people used it later than that. The significance of this is that he may have had Isaiah 54:13 in mind. There, God says through his prophet that there is going to be a day in which God will teach his own children. In the Greek translation of that verse, the words "taught" and "God" are side by side, and so, the argument goes, Paul went one step further and combined them into a single word: *Thessalonians, you are God-taught.*

> The way the Thessalonians love one another is proof to Paul that God is fulfilling his promises.

The verse about God teaching his children in Isaiah 54 is part of a prophetic passage which spoke about what was going to happen when the **new covenant** came. Under the old covenant, which was given through Moses to the Israelites, God wrote his law on tablets of stone, but the people of God failed to obey it. But the prophets said that in the day of the new covenant, God would write that law not on tablets of stone but on people's hearts (see Jeremiah 31:33; Ezekiel 11:19; 36:26). He would do so by the Holy Spirit. God himself would teach his people the way of life by inscribing it on their hearts.

So the way that the Thessalonians love one another is not only proof to Paul that God is working in their hearts but specifically proof that the Old Testament promise of a new covenant has been fulfilled. It is evident in the Thessalonians' hearts, in their lives, and in their fellowship. What an encouragement that is, to that church and to the apostle!

Brotherly Love

Next Paul moves to his two exhortations. The first of these is in the second part of 1 Thessalonians **4:10**: "But we urge you, brothers, to do this more and more." What is "this"? The beginning of **verse 9** gives the answer: everything Paul is saying here is "concerning brotherly love." This is what he is urging his brothers and sisters in Christ to do more and more. Paul is encouraging the Thessalonians—and you and me—to keep on loving and to grow in that love ever-increasingly.

This word "brotherly love" in Greek is *philadelphia*—the word which gives the city of Philadelphia its name. When philosophers in Paul's day used this word, they were always talking about family love. If a philosopher came to a town to give a lecture in ethics and he started talking about *philadelphia*, what he meant was "Families ought to love one another."

Here, Paul takes that language and extends it by applying it to the way that *Christians* love one another. We need to love one another like family. The **ethics** of family love apply to the entire Christian community.

Paul bases his exhortation to grow in this kind of love on the fact that God is already at work in this church, creating brotherly love between them. His argument is not *God is at work in you, so there's no need for me to exhort you to love one another.* No, God is at work in them so that they love one another; and *therefore* Paul is exhorting them to love one another still more.

We live in a culture where groups can be very tight-knit; yet, very often, our relations and connections are not gospel-centered. All through this letter, Paul wants us to make a priority of the gospel. This is the thing that binds us together—that makes us brothers and sisters. So it ought to express itself in our life as a community—as a family. Brotherly love means caring for one another and loving one another. However large a congregation is, it should be a family and should ever be striving to become more and more like a family, reflected in each member's love, concern, care, and commitment for the others.

This is therefore a challenge for all of us as individuals who are part of a church—in other words, for every believer, for the New Testament knows nothing of a Christian who is not part of a local church.

We need to ask ourselves:

- Do I really value as brothers and sisters—like blood kin—the people who have joined with me in **professing** Jesus Christ in my local church? Are they the people with whom I feel most at home?

- What am I doing to contribute to that family?

- And do I likewise value my brothers and sisters outside my local church?

This is Paul's challenge to each of us in verses **9-10**.

Godly Living

The second thing Paul urges the Thessalonian church toward is godly living. In the Thessalonians' case, that means three things.

First, he tells them to "aspire to live quietly" (**v 11**). They are to avoid public controversy. They are not to court attention—not to look to gather a crowd around them to watch what they do. They are just to live quietly and be faithful.

Second, Paul says, "Mind your own affairs." We might say, "Mind your own business." Christians should not be busybodies, finding out what everyone else is doing and getting involved in their lives. It is not that we shouldn't care for one another and seek to know one another deeply; but we are not to meddle just for the sake of it.

Third, Paul commands the members of this church to "work with your hands, as we instructed you." He is not telling them that office jobs are less godly than manual labor; the emphasis is on working hard and supporting themselves, whatever the job. This is clear from the end of **verse 12**: "Be dependent on no one." They should avoid being a burden on their fellow believers. So should we.

Note that this does not mean that we shouldn't allow our brothers and sisters to love and look after us. The phrase "be dependent on no one" cannot mean *cut yourself off from others* or *get through life on your own* because these things would contradict the exhortation to show brotherly love to one another in **verses 9-10**. What Paul is saying is *Don't burden others unnecessarily.* If church members need help, then they should look to their church family to provide it; but if they can support themselves, they should.

It seems from the remainder of this letter and from Paul's second letter to this church that he is seeking to address here some people who have decided that they don't have to work anymore because they know Jesus is coming again to judge the earth and take his people to be with him forever. They think they can focus on making predictions about when and how Jesus is coming back, and depend upon other people to provide for their day-to-day sustenance. The phrase "be dependent" in **verse 12** could mean depending on wealthy people in the church to take care of them; or it could mean that they have even been going out in the streets and begging in order to gain shelter and clothing—as the **Cynic philosophers** in those days did.

Paul says, *No, no, no.* As Christians we want to live a godly life—and part of that means that we are to live quietly, mind our own business, and work hard, instead of making life harder for one another.

The Great Commandment

Essentially, then, verses 1-12 can be boiled down to two exhortations: "to please God ... more and more" (v 1) and "to love one another ... more and more" (**v 9-10**).

This is not original to Paul! He is essentially quoting Jesus:

"You shall love the Lord your God with all your heart and with all your soul and with all your mind. This is the great and first commandment. And a second is like it: You shall love your neighbor as yourself. On these two commandments depend all **the Law and the Prophets**." (Matthew 22:37-39)

Paul is telling the Thessalonians to love God and to love their neighbors. They are to consciously reject living self-focused lives and live for God and one another. Why? It's partly in order to be a witness to outsiders. In 1 Thessalonians **4:12** Paul gives another reason for his concern about this kind of conduct and about brotherly love: "so that you may walk properly before outsiders." The testimony of our lives to unbelievers ought to be one of attractive witness to Jesus Christ. Paul wants us to live in such a way that we actually have that kind of testimony: that people would admire God's people because of their good conduct, and that this would lead them to place their faith in Jesus and experience the Spirit's transforming power for themselves.

Self-focused people usually live self-focused lives because they think they'll be happier. Yet they tend to be miserable. But those who follow Paul's exhortations—those who live for God and for their brothers and sisters and, in doing so, provide a good witness to the watching world—are the ones who end up knowing true joy and happiness. Living self-forgetful lives is the way God wants us to live, and it is into this kind of life that God pours out his richest blessing—which is to know him and to know his presence beside us.

Questions for reflection

1. Reflect on the questions about brotherly love on page 100. What is one thing you can do to love your Christian brothers and sisters more this week?

2. When might it be tempting for you to meddle in others' lives or to burden them unnecessarily? What would it look like for you to "live quietly"?

3. Paul's focus on loving other Christian brothers and sisters may seem inward-looking. But why is this so important for our witness and evangelism? Can you think of an example of this in your own life?

PART TWO

We have said all along that the aim of this letter is to teach Christians how to live life in light of Jesus' return. In 1 Thessalonians **4:13** Paul starts to get very specific on that topic. It seems that the Thessalonians have been asking him some questions about what happens to those who die before the Lord returns.

It's clear that in the short time that Paul was able to teach them in person, one aspect of his teaching was the second coming of Christ. This is no surprise, since it is one of the principal aspects of Christian teaching. It is, for example, found in the Apostles' Creed, a short summary of the Christian faith that began to develop in the early days of the second century, which states, "On the third day he rose again; he ascended into heaven, he is seated at the right hand of the Father, and he will come to judge the living and the dead," and "I believe in … the resurrection of the body, and the life everlasting." And, of course, the second coming of Christ is found in Jesus' teaching. In Matthew's Gospel in particular, but also in the other Gospels, Christ speaks a lot about the end times to his own disciples. The resurrection, ascension and the second coming were a central part of the gospel message from the very start.

But the Thessalonians still had some questions. They came from a culture in which the idea of resurrection was strange. When Paul was preaching on Mars Hill in Athens among the philosophers and he mentioned the resurrection, their response was *Who is this babbler?* (Acts 17:18). They mocked him as some sort of an idiot for believing in the resurrection. They found it a very strange teaching, and one that they could not accept. In the thought world of the Greco-Roman society, life after death meant only a very vague, shadowy afterlife of the soul, which was thought to exist as a shade in the underworld—nothing like the full bodily resurrection of Jesus. It is therefore not surprising that the new believers in Thessalonica should have been wrestling with the implications of the doctrine of the physical return of Christ and the resurrection. In particular, they want to know what happens to believers who die before Jesus comes again. Is there hope for them? This is the question Paul answers in 1 Thessalonians **4:13-18**; and in doing so, he gives us, as believers today, peace, hope, and joy as we look forward to his return and our own resurrection.

Truth Is for Comfort

I remember hearing years ago a story about the Canadian evangelist Leighton Ford. When his oldest son, Sandy, died in 1982 at twenty-one years of age, Ford said, "I was wrestling to bring my faith and my emotions together." Ford knew what he believed. He trusted in the Bible, and he trusted in the word of God, but he had lost his oldest son, and he found that incredibly hard.

In times of bereavement, we all have questions, including believers. *What's happened to her? Is he all right? Where is she now? Will I recognize him when I see him again?*

This is why one of the purposes of a Christian funeral service is to bring the truth of the word of God to bear on the experience of his people. And this is a passage which Christian funerals often go to. That makes perfect sense because what Paul is saying here applied not only to the Thessalonians 2,000 years ago but applies also to us. The Bible does not just teach us how to live; it teaches us how to face death.

The little phrase at the start of **verse 13** is one which Paul uses several times in his writings: "We do not want you to be uninformed." We find it in Romans 1:13; Romans 11:25; 1 Corinthians 10:1; and 1 Corinthians 12:1. It might sound like a throwaway phrase, but it is in fact very significant. It is as if Paul is drawing a big arrow that says, *This is important! Read and remember this!*

Paul is very concerned to ensure that we are not ignorant of the truth about the second coming. This is because the truth that he is going to tell us in this passage is meant for our comfort. Theology—truth about God—is what God uses to comfort, strengthen, and grow us. In this passage, the truth Paul is about to explain is intended to prevent the Thessalonians from grieving like those who have no hope (1 Thessalonians **4:13**).

Paul does not say that Christians should never grieve. He does not say that if we believe in the gospel of Christ Jesus, and therefore in the bodily resurrection and the life hereafter, then we should not be upset by death. Your grief for the loss of a believing loved one is an act of gratitude to God, who gave you the gift of that person in the first place; it is a way of honoring their memory. There is nothing wrong with grief. What Paul does say is this: *I don't want you, in your grief, to be like someone without hope.*

At the beginning of the 20th century, a German scholar named Adolf Deissmann uncovered some letters from about the time of the New Testament. One was a letter written in Greek by a woman named Irene, offering words of sympathy and condolence to two friends who had just lost a loved one. What she wrote is very striking when we compare it to what Paul was able to write. Irene wrote, "Against such things one can do nothing. Therefore, comfort one another" (*Light from the Ancient East*, p 164).

Do you find that comforting—the idea that you really can't do anything about death? I don't. This is the attitude, prevalent in the culture of his day, that Paul is describing to the Thessalonians. He doesn't want them to be hopeless like Irene in her letter. Rather, he wants them to be hope-filled.

When Jesus Returns

Paul cites two truths in **verse 14**—one past, one future—which provide us with hope in the hour of death; namely, Jesus has risen again, and so will we.

"For since we believe that Jesus died and rose again, even so, through Jesus, God will bring with him those who have fallen asleep."

Paul is saying to these believers that what happened to their Savior will happen to them. If any believer is not alive on the day when Jesus comes again—if they have "fallen asleep"—then they will be raised from death just as he was raised.

This goes for every believer who has ever lived and died or who will ever live and die, until that final generation who will still be alive when Jesus comes again. Assuming we are not part of that last generation, we are all going to die, but we are also all going to be raised from death just as Jesus was raised from death. Our hope is grounded in the bodily resurrection of Jesus Christ. As the hymn puts it:

Jesus lives and so shall I.
Death, thy sting is gone forever:
He, who deigned for me to die,
Lives, the bands of death to sever.
He shall raise me with the just;
Jesus is my hope and trust.

(Christian F. Gellert, translated by John Dunmore Lang)

Because Jesus was raised from the dead bodily, the sting of death is gone forever. He died so that, for those who trust in him, death is simply a portal into glory. Perhaps that's why Paul doesn't say, "those who have died" but "those who have fallen asleep." Death isn't permanent. When we face the death of our loved ones, we can be comforted by the fact that Jesus died, was buried, and was bodily raised again from the dead; and so therefore they will be too.

It's clear from **verse 16** that our physical resurrection will come when Jesus returns and not before then: "The Lord himself will descend from heaven ... And the dead in Christ will rise." So the question arises: what happens to the dead between now and that moment? Some commentators see the phrase "fallen asleep" and read into it the idea that after we die, we enter what they call "soul sleep"—a kind of unconscious hibernation phase. I think they take "fallen asleep" too literally. Elsewhere in the Bible it's clear that the existence we have immediately after we die is not like an unconscious sleeping state. In Luke 16 Jesus gives a parable about a rich man and a poor man and their experiences after death. He tells us, "The poor man died and was carried by the angels to Abraham's side. The rich man also died and was buried, and in **Hades**, being in torment, he lifted up his eyes and saw Abraham far off" (v 22-23). It's clear that both have a conscious existence—one happy and blessed, the other in torment. Along the same lines, Paul tells us that "to die is gain ... My desire is to depart and be with Christ, for that is far better" (Philippians 1:21, 23). Paul expects to die and immediately be with Christ. It therefore makes most sense to read "fallen asleep" in 1 Thessalonians **4:14** as simply a metaphor for dying.

But our state immediately after we die is not Paul's main focus here. He is really interested in the bodily resurrection that will happen when Jesus comes again. In **verses 15-17** he goes on to give more details about this resurrection, again with the purpose of encouraging and comforting the Thessalonian Christians. They had apparently been wondering whether those believers who die before Jesus comes again are going to be left out, or left behind, when he does. Paul's answer to them is *No—they're going to be first in line!*

> We won't be floating around as ethereal beings; it will be a real, physical resurrection.

Paul has had a specific "word from the Lord" about this (**v 15**); he is speaking with the authority that God has given him as an apostle. He explains that those who are alive when Jesus comes again "will not precede those who have fallen asleep" (**v 15**). Actually, "the dead in Christ will rise first" (**v 16**); then those who are alive "will be caught up together with them in the clouds to meet the Lord in the air" (**v 17**). It's a grand vision. Think of it! The countless throngs of those who have died trusting in Jesus throughout history, suddenly fully risen with new bodies, and those believers who still wait on the earth rising to meet their Lord at last.

This isn't floating around as an ethereal being in heaven for eternity; it's a real, physical, bodily resurrection.

With God Forever

I love the phrase at the end of **verse 17**: "We will always be with the Lord." This is the greatest comfort of all. I'm often asked by people in the hour of death, "Where is heaven?" And my answer is this: "I don't know where heaven is, but I do know that all those who trust in Jesus are going to be with Jesus forever. Wherever Jesus is, there is heaven, and we're going to be with him forever."

Paul, too, recognizes that this is a hugely encouraging truth. In **verse 18**, he says, "Encourage one another with these words." As they struggle with bereavement, these Christians need to bring the word of God to bear on their experience. Even in the valley of the shadow of death, they will find comfort and strength as they realize that they will always be with the Lord, reunited with their loved ones who fell asleep trusting that same Lord.

Often, after a funeral or at a graveside service, someone will say to me, "I just don't know what people do who don't have Christ and who don't believe the gospel. I don't know how they handle this." I always reply, "I don't know either. I'm so thankful we have Christ and we have the gospel."

Paul is telling us to encourage one another with that truth, even in the valley of the shadow of death.

There was a man named Al in the church in Jackson where I served as pastor, who did a wonderful job of giving people words of encouragement. He would send people Scriptures which brought the word of God to bear on their lives. We needed it, and we still need it. You and I live in a world filled with troubles. Even in the most godly, wonderful Christian homes, there is heartbreak and grief. We need the encouragement of the truth of God in the word of God: of rich, sound biblical theology. And it is often in times of pain and difficulty that it becomes hardest to remember and live by the truths of the gospel, even when we have known them for years. This is why Paul calls us to "encourage one another with these words." We must take the truth of the word of God and use it to encourage one another in the hour of death and bereavement. We have more than empty platitudes to offer; we have certain hope.

The Lord Jesus Christ did that on the night before he was crucified. In John 14, his disciples were filled with anxiety. In fact, they were filled with foreboding. They knew something was wrong—that something was about to happen that was not going to be good. But Jesus said to them, "Let not your hearts be troubled" (John 14:1). And how did he encourage them not to have troubled hearts? What truth did he speak of?

"Believe in God; believe also in me. In my Father's house are many rooms. If it were not so, would I have told you that I go to prepare a place for you? And if I go and prepare a place for you, I will come again and will take you to myself, that where I am you may be also." (v 1-3)

Jesus connected the disciples' trouble to the truth of his future return. "I will come again and will take you to myself, that where I am you may be also." This truth is what would give them comfort. Belief in God *and knowledge of our future resurrection life with our Lord is* what answers the anxieties of our souls.

Questions for reflection

1. What questions have you heard people ask about our future after we die? How might this passage help you to answer some of those questions?

2. What comfort is there in this passage for those who grieve?

3. Why does looking forward to the second coming help us with the anxieties of each day?

8. CHILDREN OF LIGHT

1 Thessalonians 5 is where Paul begins to tackle his key theme of the return of Christ head-on. The question here is: how do you prepare for the return of Christ? That is what the Thessalonians want to know. Specifically, it seems that they are interested in trying to nail down the timing of Christ's return.

That makes sense as a question. Surely it would help you to prepare for the return of Christ if you knew when that was going to be. But Paul gives them a very definite answer to that question—the same answer that Jesus gave to his disciples— which is that we cannot know when Christ will return. After that, Paul goes on to tell the Thessalonians about the way in which believers *should* go about preparing for the return of Jesus Christ. We prepare ourselves not by predictions about when Jesus is coming but by the pursuit of godliness.

Inevitable but Unpredictable

The first thing that Paul says is that prognostication is not the way to prepare for Jesus' return. "Concerning the times and the seasons, brothers, you have no need to have anything written to you" (**v 1**).

Clearly the Thessalonians have said to Paul something like, *We'd like to hear more from you about the timing of Jesus' return.* But he knows they actually don't need him to write to them about that.

Jesus had already told his disciples that his coming would be like the coming of a thief in the night. In Matthew 24:3, the disciples asked, "Tell us, when will these things be, and what will be the sign of your coming and of **the end of the age**?" But Jesus responded only with "Concerning that day and hour no one knows, not even the angels of heaven, nor the Son, but the Father only" (v 36).

Here's a tip for us: when Jesus tells us that even *he* doesn't know something, it is probably sensible to drop trying to figure it out ourselves! In his letter to the Thessalonians, Paul is essentially repeating what Jesus said. They don't need to know when Jesus will return. In fact, this is something which is not given to any of us to know, including Jesus.

> It is more certain that Jesus will return than that the sun will rise tomorrow.

Paul goes on: "You yourselves are fully aware that the day of the Lord will come like a thief in the night" (1 Thessalonians **5:2**). Again, this language comes right from what Jesus said to the disciples: "Know this, that if the master of the house had known in what part of the night the thief was coming, he would have stayed awake and would not have let his house be broken into. Therefore you also must be ready, for the **Son of Man** is coming at an hour you do not expect" (Matthew 24:43-44; the same image is used in Luke 12:39-40). The point of this image is unpredictability. If you could predict exactly when thieves would come, it would be pointless for them to try and break into your home.

The Lord's return is inevitable but unpredictable. Paul makes that very clear here. The occurrence of Jesus' coming is absolutely certain. It is more certain that Jesus is going to return than it is that the sun is going to rise tomorrow. But the *timing* of it is uncertain—just as uncertain as the timing of the arrival of a thief.

Paul emphasizes in the following verses that the second coming is going to be sudden and surprising, especially for unbelievers. Notice the language that he uses in 1 Thessalonians **5:3**: "sudden destruction" will come, like labor pains upon a pregnant woman. It doesn't make any difference at all whether you believe it's coming or not—

it'll happen. Paul's words are very serious. "They [unbelievers] will not escape."

We live in a time and place in which very few people—outside of the church—have any kind of anticipation of a reckoning with God at the end, a real belief in a returning Savior who will judge the living and the dead. Many people in our Western world have confidence in a purely scientific understanding of the world, one whereby we can predict and aim to control what will happen. Scientists tell us that 6 billion years from now, give or take a few, our world will implode upon itself; but that doesn't seem very urgent! Even the more pessimistic of climate-change predictions don't anticipate the total, sudden destruction which Paul describes in this verse—and they certainly don't predict a day of judgment. This attitude seeps into the minds of believers, surrounded as we are by that worldview. It produces a lack of belief that Jesus is really coming back and that the world as we know it will really, suddenly come to an end.

But belief in the second coming is a core part of the Christian faith—and not only expecting it to happen but also longing for it. The day of judgment will be not only a day of destruction but also a day on which all wrongs will be righted, sin and death will be no more, and those who have trusted in Jesus will begin to dwell with him eternally. It will be a wonderful day. The second-to-last verse in the Bible says, "Come, Lord Jesus!" (Revelation 22:20). Judgment and salvation may not come when we expect, but they are certainly coming, as surely as a pregnant woman will experience labor pains.

Children of Light

So, Christians are not to prepare for the Lord's coming by trying to figure out the date on which it will happen. But in verses 4 and 5, Paul moves on to say that there *is* a way in which we can be prepared.

"But you are not in darkness, brothers, for that day to surprise you like a thief" (1 Thessalonians **5:4**). Even though we don't know when exactly Jesus will return, it is still possible for Christians to live in a state of readiness so that we won't be taken by surprise when that day comes. When Paul uses the word "darkness" here, he means moral darkness. The Thessalonian Christians are not in the deadness of sin and the grave of unrighteousness, as the world is. They have seen the light of salvation in Christ. Paul repeats this again in **verse 5**: they are "children of light, children of the day ... not of the night or of the darkness." Being children of light means we know the truth. We know God, and we have been saved by Jesus.

Because we are not in the dark, Paul says, we should "keep awake and be sober." In other words, the way to get ready for Jesus' return is by the pursuit of godliness: that is, by the life of faith.

In Jesus' parable in Matthew 24, he said, "If the master of the house had known in what part of the night the thief was coming, he would have stayed awake and would not have let his house be broken into" (v 43). Paul uses the same metaphor here when he says, "Let us not sleep, as others do, but let us keep awake" (1 Thessalonians **5:6**). Be ready; be awake; be watchful.

This is not being watchful for signs of the timing of Jesus' return. This watchfulness is of a different sort. It means living life in anticipation of the return of Christ—living a life in which the hope of the second coming directs and governs everything else. We will live very differently from someone who thinks that this life is all there is. We will avoid overvaluing things that are going to pass away and instead live for what "neither moth nor rust destroys" (Matthew 6:20)—the kingdom of God. We will not despair when we encounter injustice and pain, but we can address these things in the confidence that there is going to be a day when Jesus comes again to settle all accounts and right all wrongs, and when this world will be transformed into the new heavens and the new earth.

Do you live that way? Do you know others who live that way? Believers like that are encouraging for other Christians to be around. They allow us to see things in a different way so that we don't get trapped by the world's concerns. They live for Jesus; they live for his return. That is the kind of watchfulness that Paul is talking about.

Second, Paul tells us to "be sober" (1 Thessalonians **5:6**). This is not an indication that the Thessalonians had a problem with drunkenness. If this were a letter to the Corinthians, we might think so; but there's no indication that the Thessalonians had been abusing alcohol. It is a metaphor—an illustration. Paul clarifies this in **verse 7**: "Those who get drunk, are drunk at night."

The last time I preached on this passage, a woman met me at the door afterwards and said, "I'm a trauma nurse, and I see all sorts of bad things happen at night." She understood first-hand why Paul had chosen to use this metaphor to describe immoral living. Didn't our mothers always tell us to stay out of trouble and come home before it got dark? The general principle is: bad things happen at night because it's easy to hide. Paul is using the night, which is when people get drunk and violence increases, to help us understand what spiritual darkness looks like.

So we should be "sober" instead. He repeats this again in **verse 8**: "Since we belong to the day, let us be sober." It is an indication that Christians are to be self-controlled. We are to use the things of this world in moderation. It's another

> The attitude is out there (and sometimes in the church) that the one who dies with the most toys wins.

way of saying what we saw above: live in a way that is in line with the light, not in a way that is in line with the darkness. Live for Jesus, not for the world.

If someone thinks this world is all there is, they will try to grab as much of it as they can—whether or not they are professing Christians. There used to be a beer commercial on television that encouraged us to "go for the gusto" because "you only go around once in life." That attitude is out there (and sometimes, if we are honest, in the church too); the one who dies with the most toys wins. But Christians must be sober, moderate, and self-controlled in the way we use the things of this world because we know that this is not all there is, and we know that the things of the world are not the most important things, nor will they last forever. We must learn to use the world and love the Lord, not love the world and use the Lord.

Questions for reflection

1. "Belief in the second coming is a core part of the Christian faith." How do you respond to that statement? Are there ways in which you could take the second coming more seriously?

2. What stops you from living watchfully? How could you remind yourself to live for Jesus and not for the world's concerns?

3. What do you think it means to "love the world and use the Lord"? How can we avoid this?

PART TWO

The second half of this section, which focuses very specifically on what it means to be ready for the return of Christ, continues with a concluding word on how we are to pursue godliness (**v 8**). After that, Paul shows us what the great prize of the Christian life is—which will make all the difference in preparing for the coming of the Lord (**v 9-10**). Finally, in **verse 11** he tells us that we need to encourage one another in these things—in the truths which he has taught from **verse 4** all the way down to **verse 10**. They need to be worked into our hearts, into our lives, and into the very fabric of who we are so that we are prepared for the return of Christ.

Armed and Ready

In **verse 8** Paul calls us to cultivate faith, love, and hope.

First, we are to "put on the breastplate of faith." We live by faith: that is, we live by believing in the word of God, trusting in the promises of God, and putting our trust in the person of the Lord Jesus Christ. Much of the life of faith is learning to trust the Lord with all our hearts and lean not on our own understanding (Proverbs 3:5). The minute that we start to measure this life only by what we experience, feel, and see, and not in accordance with God's word, we will go wrong.

This shows itself most clearly, perhaps, when tragedy strikes in life. Every time somebody dies or some terrible crime is committed—people will say something like "How can you still believe in the mercy of God in light of what has happened?" And if we base our understanding of the love of God solely on what we see in the world, then we will be deeply confused and discouraged.

It was ever thus. If you had been standing on that hill outside of Jerusalem watching what Jesus' mother and his disciples saw on the afternoon of the crucifixion, and you hadn't had the Scriptures to tell you what was going on, would you have drawn the conclusion that God was, in his love and grace and mercy, saving the souls of billions? Of course not. You would have looked at the cross, and you would have said, "This is the victory of hate and spite and envy and bitterness. This is a good man who's been crushed by the political and religious machine. There's no justice in this world." But the Bible teaches you to look at that cross differently. In the same way, it teaches you to look at all of life differently.

Faith is taking God at his word, even when circumstances suggest a different view.

The life of faith is learning to take God at his word, even at times when the evidence of circumstances suggests a different view. It is trusting that God, who has always been faithful, will continue to be so. It is believing that he is at work in even the most difficult and painful of situations. It is looking forward to the day when Jesus returns and makes all things right. If we want to be ready for Jesus' return, we must live by the Bible. That is what it means to "put on the breastplate of faith."

But this is not just a breastplate of faith but also, second, of love (**verse 8**). We are to cultivate an attitude of love. This is the greatest commandment. Right before Jesus was betrayed, taken captive, put through an illegal trial, and crucified, one of the last things he said to his disciples was "Love one another as I have loved you" (John 15:12). This is his command. So, if we want to show him that we love him, then we should obey it.

Very simply, we are to be loving people. We are to love God and love one another; we are to love our neighbor, our fellow Christians, our spouse, and even our enemy (Matthew 5:44). This is not easy: we are being called to love sinners, and sinners hurt us even when we are trying to love them (just as we will in turn hurt those who love us). But living a life of love is how to be ready for his return.

Third, there is hope. Paul explains in his letter to the Romans what the Christian hope is. First, he says what we hope for: "We wait eagerly for adoption as sons, the redemption of our bodies" (Romans 8:23). That is, we hope for the return of Jesus, the resurrection of the dead, and the eternal life we have been promised in Christ. Second, Paul explains what hope looks like: "For in this hope we were saved. Now hope that is seen is not hope. For who hopes for what he sees? But if we hope for what we do not see, we wait for it with patience" (v 24-25).

Suppose you're standing on a street corner waiting for some friends to come and meet you. You're hoping they will come soon; you're patiently and expectantly waiting. That's hope. That's what we feel with regard to Jesus' return. It's a sure and certain hope, not wishful thinking: Jesus has promised to come, and he keeps his promises! But we have to wait patiently because we don't know when he'll come; we can't see him on the horizon yet. This patient waiting is the hope that Paul tells us to put on as a helmet.

It's significant that he uses this armor imagery. Paul could just tell us plainly to live lives of faith, love, and hope—but he doesn't. "Put on the breastplate of faith and love, and for a helmet the hope of salvation." The point is that these things protect us. We need them to overcome the deadly arrows of the evil one (Ephesians 6:16). The world will tell us that Jesus is not coming back, that death is the end, and that we should live for ourselves. How do we protect ourselves from becoming sucked in by the world's way of thinking? How do we prepare for Jesus' coming? We live by faith, we live in love, and we live with hope.

Living with Jesus

Next, Paul tells us something very important about why Jesus died. There is not just one biblical answer to the question: what did Jesus' death accomplish? Jesus' death accomplished untold blessings for his people. He removed our sin (John 1:29); he redeemed us from the curse of the law (Galatians 3:13-14); he overcame the powers of evil (Colossians 2:15); he made us his people (1 Peter 2:10)—and that's just the beginning. 1 Thessalonians **5:9-10** highlights another of these blessings: our Lord Jesus Christ died for us *so that we might live with him.*

Jesus saved us *from* God's wrath against sin (**v 9**)—but what did he save us *for*? "That whether we are awake or asleep we might live with him" (**v 10**). Paul is saying that fellowship with Jesus is what he died to give us. He died so that we might be his and he ours forever. That is the great blessing, the great treasure in life. No temporary pleasure or blessing in this world could possibly substitute for that eternal blessing of fellowship with Jesus.

Jesus is not just a get-out clause or a means to an end. He is the end. He is the goal; he is the point; he is the prize.

Realizing this motivates us to be—and to stay—ready for his return. If I am living for something earthly, Jesus' coming is going to be bad news for me because I will have to give that thing up. But you and I will never have to give Jesus up. The missionary Jim Elliot, quoting one of the Puritans, famously said, "He is no fool who gives up what he cannot keep to gain what he cannot lose." Paul is saying the same thing here. You cannot lose Jesus. He is forever. The reason he died is so that you would have him and he would have you forever. We must never prize anything in this life more than that.

This is Paul's main point in these verses; but there is more. In **verse 10**, Paul says that Christ died so that we might live with him "whether we are awake or asleep." This is a metaphor for "whether we are alive or dead." Paul is not using this language in the sense in which he used it in 5:6-7—morality and the life of faith versus immorality and the life of sin—but in the sense in which he used it in 4:15. He is reminding the Thessalonians of his previous point: that those who have already died when Jesus returns will still be included in the last day. All who trust in Christ, whether or not they have already died, will be raised on the judgment day and live with Jesus forever.

This is reminiscent of what Paul says in Philippians 1: "Christ will be honored in my body, whether by life or by death. For to me to live is Christ, and to die is gain ... My desire is to depart and be with Christ, for that is far better" (Philippians 1:20-21, 23). Even when we are dead, we are in Christ. What a great hope! This means that when we face the death of a loved one who is trusting in Christ or find ourselves diagnosed with serious illness, we don't need to be consumed by fears for the future or regrets from the past. We have lived in Christ—redeemed, forgiven, and indwelled by his Spirit—and we die in Christ, gaining resurrection life with him forever. When all else fails, even our own breath, Jesus our Savior is there. "Whether we are awake or asleep we ... live with him."

Encourage One Another with These Things

Paul finishes this section by exhorting the Thessalonians to "encourage one another and build one another up" (1 Thessalonians **5:11**). The truths he has outlined about Jesus' return and how we are to live in light of it are the very things we should encourage one another with.

I have four Scottish friends who are a great encouragement to me: Ian and Allison Macleod and Murdo and Emma Macleod. From the world's standpoint these couples have it all. Both Ian and Murdo are high-ranking attorneys in their fields; Allison is a medical doctor and Emma is a university professor. People would look at them and say, "They've got it all." Yet these qualifications—the things that the world looks at and admires—are not the things that Ian and Allison and Murdo and Emma count most important. They treasure Jesus more than anything. Just being around them and seeing them live a life in which they treasure Jesus more than anything is a huge encouragement to me. And I could say the same of about 500 other families I know.

We often don't realize that we can be an encouragement and a support to one another simply by living as though this world is not all that there is: by living out the truth that there's something more important than the things that the people around us clamor for. You can build someone up in their faith simply by valuing Jesus more than anything this world can give.

We live in danger of the acid of unbelief in the world seeping into our souls and robbing us of joy because it destroys our true perspective and stops us from living for what we ought to live for. But when we see someone refusing to listen to the unbelief of the world—when we see someone living determinedly for Jesus with all they have—we are spurred on to do the same. We can encourage one another not only by reminding each other verbally of the truths in this chapter—that Christ died for us, that he rose again, that he will return one day, that the dead will be raised, and that we will live with him forever—but also by living out those truths in our day-to-day lives.

Our God is so kind. He doesn't say, *I saved you; now for the rest you are on your own.* He provides us with all that we need as we wait for his coming. He provides us with the Spirit, who sanctifies us, and he provides us with one another as an encouragement. We are each to open ourselves up to receiving that kind of encouragement from those who live in light of Jesus' return, putting their hope not in this world but in the next; and we are to commit ourselves to providing that kind of encouragement to our brothers and sisters in our turn, as we live in that way too.

Questions for reflection

1. What could faith, love, and hope protect you from in your life this week—and what would it look like for you to put that armor on?

2. Do you ever think of Jesus' salvation as a get-out clause? How does it encourage you to think that he died so that "we might live with him"?

3. Who could you encourage and build up this week, either by your actions or with a truth from this chapter?

9. BEING THE CHURCH

"Christian Community" and "How to Be a Gospel Church" are the titles which John Stott gives to 1 Thessalonians 5:12-28 in his wonderful commentary on 1 and 2 Thessalonians in the *Bible Speaks Today* series. Those are both great titles for this section. In this chapter we'll look just at **verses 12-15**, which contain either eight or ten exhortations from Paul, depending on how you count! Stott explains that these exhortations teach us first, "how pastors and people ... should relate to and regard one another," and second, "about the responsibilities of church members to care for each other" (*The Message of Thessalonians*, p 118). Then, in the final section of 1 Thessalonians 5, which we'll look at in the next chapter, Paul turns our attention to "the nature and conduct of public worship" (p 124). These three considerations together are the fundamental ones for building a gospel church.

So first, in **verses 12-13**, Paul tells the Thessalonians to respect, esteem, and love their elders, who labor, lead, and admonish them. There are six things in this one sentence! This is Paul's exhortation about how people and pastors are to relate.

The last time this text was in the preaching program at the church where I used to serve as pastor, a congregation member saw it coming and said, "Isn't it going to be kind of awkward for you to preach a sermon to the congregation about how we are supposed to respect and love you more?" But actually, that is not quite Paul's message. He is not talking about the Thessalonians' behavior and attitude toward him but about the way they treat their leaders in their own local congregation. So when I preached this text, I tried to follow Paul's example and focus the attention not on me but on all the other leaders in our local congregation.

This passage does not use the word "elder" or "pastor," but those are the people we should understand Paul to be talking about. These are those "who labor among you and are over you in the Lord and admonish you" (**v 12**). Those three things are what the elders of a church do—they labor, they lead, and they teach their congregations. "Admonish" is the Greek word *noutheteo*, which can mean "warn" or "caution" but literally means "put in mind"—so it doesn't mean "admonish" in the sense of "tell off" but rather, speaks of the pastor or elder's work in reminding others of what they know and what impact it should have in their lives. We see the same three things in 1 Timothy 5:17: "Let the elders who rule well be considered worthy of double honor, especially those who labor in preaching and teaching." Ruling or leading, laboring, and teaching or admonishing are three key duties of any elder or pastor.

It is notable that 1 Thessalonians is one of the earliest books (if not the very earliest) of the New Testament, and Paul is already talking about the duties of the eldership—those who lead a church. That shouldn't surprise us: the book of Acts describes how Paul made sure that elders had been ordained to lead the fledgling churches in the regions he'd visited (Acts 14:23). This followed a pattern that stretched all the way back to the Old Testament, not just in the days of the synagogue but all the way back to Moses (Numbers 11:16). Godly leadership is and has always been intrinsic to the shepherding and flourishing of God's people. So before we turn to Paul's exhortation to the congregation members in Thessalonica, it is worth pausing to look at these three duties of church leaders.

Work Hard

A mother in my former congregation once told me that she had overheard her son saying to her husband, "I wish that you could have a job like Dr. Duncan so that you could be with your family more. You know, he only has to work on Sunday!" There are a lot of people who think of the pastoral ministry in that way. But effective, godly pastoral work proves to be hard work six days a week, and it should be. The word translated "labor" here is a strong word. Paul is not speaking of light work but rather, sweat-inducing labor. It is typical of Paul to talk in this way. Elsewhere, when he describes the work of ministry, he uses words for the toil that farmers go through in planting and plowing and harvesting, and illustrations of soldiers and athletes, to describe the kind of work that he has in mind (e.g. 2 Timothy 2:1-6).

Unfortunately, pastoral ministry *can* be a place for lazy men to hide in, doing the bare minimum. But that is not Paul's vision for pastoral ministry—nor should it be our ambition or expectation for it. If you are a pastor or an elder, I say to you: brother, let us labor together, let us sweat together, let us toil together. It's worth noting that the Reformer John Calvin said in his commentary on 1 Thessalonians 5:12, "From this it follows that all idle bellies are excluded from the number of pastors."

The hallmark of any real ministry must be a dedicated work ethic. If you are in ministry, and are not sweating and toiling and working hard with joy in your heart, it is not the kind of gospel pastoral ministry that the Bible lays out.

Lead with Care

Second, Paul is speaking of those who "are over you." This leadership is not harsh authoritarianism. Nor is it simply a question of who takes the lead, as good fathers do for their families. Church leaders are there to actively guide and shepherd their congregations.

That is the language which Paul used in his speech to the Ephesian elders in Acts 20:28. They were "overseers" of a "flock," and their role was to "care for the church of God." A minister's role used to be called "the cure of souls," which means caring for people's eternal well-being. That is what Paul expects church leaders to especially care about: the eternal well-being of their congregation.

If you are a ministry leader, let me encourage you constantly to think about eternal matters: the eternal destinies and the eternal well-being of your people. They are surrounded on every side by a thousand cares and details of life—so much so sometimes that they can forget the things that will last forever. As ministers, we are called to constantly hold eternal things before those eyes and to think about the eternal destiny of those people. There will be a day when church leaders will stand and give an account to the Lord Jesus of their ministry in the midst of his people (Hebrews 13:17). We should make it our desire and prayer that we will stand on that day knowing that we have spent all that we can spend of ourselves in watching over their souls.

And if you are a church member, then let me encourage you to prize and praise leaders who do this for you. You need them to, and you need to place yourself under them as they point you to the Lord Jesus and exhort you to follow him.

Admonish and Teach

Third, church leaders are there to "admonish." As we saw above, this is not a harsh word. This type of "putting in mind" does involve confrontation when necessary, to be sure. It has a big-brotherly tone; in other words, it is kind and full of care, but it carries weight and authority. Elders are to say, "The word of God calls us to this way of life. It calls us to do *these* things; it calls us not to do *those* things." Church leaders are to teach with authority and confront when necessary, all with a view to caring for people's eternal well-being.

Most of all, this means holding the gospel up before people's eyes and hearts. The word of the cross should be the constant theme of every church and leader. Jesus is all we have—and he is more than enough. His is the power of God for salvation (Romans 1:16).

A few years ago, I was talking with a **deacon** at the church where I was then the minister. His son had been in another US state and had visited various churches, and he was recounting his experiences to his father. Of one particular congregation, he said, "There was something missing there, but I can't quite put my finger on it." His father asked him, "At any point in the service, did they say, 'This is the word of God' or 'We're going to hear the word of God' or 'We believe in the authority or the **infallibility** of the word of God'?" And his son said, "No, they never said that." His father's response was, "Ah-ha!" That was what was missing.

Our friends and fellow Christians should know that we believe every word of God's book and that we are ready to live and die by it. And this must be truer of leaders than anyone else in a church. They must, Paul says, lead not only with labor but by teaching the word of God.

How to Treat Leaders

These verses have much to tell us about the roles of a church leader, but Paul's main point is actually not an exhortation to the leaders but to the members. We are to respect, esteem, and love our church leaders.

It seems likely that the elders in Thessalonica have been involved in addressing some touchy situations in the congregation, and there has been some blow-back. It appears that people have been (or have been tempted to be) less than respectful toward their leaders. This is why Paul outlines all that church elders do; he is reminding the Thessalonian Christians of *why* their leaders ought to be treated in this way. He is calling on the congregation to show a due regard for the leaders whom the Lord has put among and over them, and who labor so hard to teach and lead them.

Our Western culture does not help us to obey this command. Ours is not a culture that loves or trusts authority and authority figures—quite the reverse. This is a fairly recent development; if we could go back in time and tell our great-grandparents about the way our generation speaks about people in authority today, I think they would all be horrified! Of course, not all leaders deserve to be respected. We can all think of leaders of recent decades—both within and outside the church—who did not labor selflessly for others, did not uphold the word of God, and even led others into grave sin and error. Brave men and women have fought against such so-called authorities for the sake of the gospel and the people of God. Still, we should recognize that our culture has an unusual disregard for and distrust of author- ity. We need to be especially careful to make sure that our attitude to authority is being shaped by the gospel, not by our culture.

> We need to be careful that our attitude to authority is shaped by the gospel, not our culture.

Jesus lived as a man under authority. He said to his disciples, "My food is to do the will of him who sent me" (John 4:34). He loved to be under the author- ity of his heavenly Father; he loved to do the work of his heavenly Father. Paul is calling on us to have the same atti- tude toward those who are in authority over us. The elders he describes in 1 Thessalonians **5:12** are "over you in the Lord"—that is, their authority doesn't stem from themselves but has been given to them by God. This gives us a clue as to what to do when we fear that our leaders are getting things wrong. Even the best, most dedicated church leaders are fallible; they may overstretch their authority, demanding more than the word of God demands, or they may wander into error in what they teach. We should remember that whatever authority they have over us comes from the Lord—and therefore must be in line with the Bible. If someone is "over us in the Lord," that means we should treat them with the utmost respect, but it also means we can challenge them when they stray from what the Lord has revealed in his word.

We are not only to respect our elders but also to "esteem them very highly in love because of their work." That means to acknowledge and think highly of their labor. It means to value them and to regard them highly because of their work. It means to love them—to let your heart be knit with them so that you care about them and have genu- ine concern for them and their families. Pray for them and tell them you are doing so; encourage them by turning up to church meetings and engaging well with their sermons; invite them over. If we love our leaders well, we will encourage them always, and respect and esteem them—then even the hardest aspects of ministry will seem well worth it and become rewarding. That brings as much benefit to a congregation as it does to its ministers.

After all, the work of leading a church is quite a work. John Calvin summarizes it in these beautiful words:

"This work is the edification of the Church, the everlasting salvation of souls, the restoration of the world, and … the kingdom of God and Christ."

(*Commentaries on the Epistle of Paul to the Philippians, Colossians, and Thessalonians*, translated by John Pringle)

If that will not drive a man to his knees, nothing will! God could have built his kingdom by himself without our aid, but in his kindness he uses weak, sinful, fallible humans to lead his church. It is a work that is far more glorious than we are.

Questions for reflection

1. If you are a church leader, what particular challenge and encouragement do these verses of 1 Thessalonians hold for you?

2. If you are a church member, what do you appreciate most about your church leaders? What could you pray for them in response to this passage?

3. What is one thing you can do this week to show your love and esteem for a leader (or co-leader) in your church?

PART TWO

In the gospel, we are brought together as family—as brothers and sisters (**v 14**).

To be a gospel church means, in the first place, that you have been brought together by the gospel. You wouldn't be a part of your congregation if it were not for the grace of God to you in the gospel and your Spirit-enabled response of faith in the claims of the gospel. Christians realize that God is our Maker and we owe worship to him. We also realize that sin is our failure; we have sinned and rebelled against him, and we deserve his condemnation. Third, we realize that Christ is our Savior—the only Savior that there is—and that he came to die in our place that we might be reconciled to God. And finally we realize that we must rest on and trust in Jesus Christ alone for salvation and that new life flows from that saving faith. That's what brings a church together: we are living together in that new life, having been freed from the bondage of sin.

It is particularly wonderful to hear Paul—"of the people of Israel, of the tribe of Benjamin, a **Hebrew** of Hebrews" (Philippians 3:5)—speaking to these Gentile Greeks in Thessalonica who'd been raised in a pagan culture and calling them "brothers" (**v 14**). It is a testament to how the gospel had brought them together. There was nothing in their heritage, in their ethnicity, or in their religious background that would have brought Paul and these Greeks together—but the gospel had. Christ brought them together so fully that Paul could call these Greek believers his "brothers."

Being Family

The gospel-shaped church should be like a family because it *is* a family. It can be very hard, frankly, to put this into practice. It's hard to know one another. It's hard to keep up with people and really be involved in their lives, and it often means we have to go an extra mile in order to really be like a family as a congregation. But it's something that we should aspire to and work toward.

A gospel church is a family, loved and chosen by God, drawing its life from God and manifesting that in the **graces** of the Christian life, especially love. That is the overarching theme of **verses 12-15**: how Christian love is manifested in our relationships. We have already looked at the relationships between pastors and people—between the elders and the congregation. Now we turn to Paul's general aspirations for the life of the church. First, in **verse 13**, there is a general instruction to be at peace with one another; second, in **verse 14**, there is the way we relate particularly to different kinds of people in the congregation; and third, in **verse 15**, there is the way we build a community that's characterized by forgiveness and kindness. All of this is about the application of Christian love.

In these verses there is not one exhortation that we can obey on our own. They all require us to relate to other people. This expresses a truth which often comes up in the New Testament and that we have noted before—we cannot grow in grace, and cannot become more mature in Christ, without one another. We can't grow to Christian maturity apart from one another because so much of our growth is in our relationships with one another—in the heartbreak of being let down and having to forgive; in the difficulty of having to walk alongside friends in Christ who are under enormous burdens; in the give and take of normal life where we defer to one another and seek to serve one another and bear with one another, and all of those other dynamics of life.

It is not so different from a biological family. In families, people get on one another's nerves and have to learn to forgive. Families can be places of tension and contention. It takes effort to be a loving family. And when it comes to a local church, Paul encourages us to strive to be a family that is shaped by the gospel. In these verses, he is telling us what that looks like.

Pursue Peace and Unity

After he finishes telling the Thessalonians to respect and love their leaders, Paul gives a second aspiration for the church at the end of **verse 13**: "Be at peace among yourselves."

Peace and unity do not just happen. They take deliberate commitment. I have served in a church where part of the membership vow was (in fact, still is) to strive for the purity and peace of the church. This is a very important part of the vow because peace has to be cultivated; and it can't be cultivated unless members aspire to it and value it. This kind of peace is not just a lack of dissension but real, positive spiritual unity—the kind that is only possible within the church.

It is expressed well in the hymn "Blest Be the Tie That Binds" by John Fawcett, especially its second stanza:

Before our Father's throne,
We pour our ardent prayers;
Our fears, our hopes, our aims are one—
Our comforts and our cares.

In a unified church family, our hearts long for the same thing. Our aspirations and aims are unified. Think about your church: Is this kind of unity what you see there? And how could you strive for it? You have to work to really be unified around one mission, one goal, one cause, and one aspiration in a local congregation. And Paul is calling us to that here.

Each Kind of Family Member

It's amazing how different the members of one family can be. If you have several children, as they grow up, you begin to see very, very different aspects of their characters and personalities emerge. It is like that in a local church too; it comprises very different kinds of people. In **verse 14**, Paul outlines how Christians should respond appropriately to each different kind of family member.

First, we are to "admonish the idle." This word "idle" is a military term referring to somebody who is out of step with the other soldiers marching in the rank. Paul says that what we need to do with this kind of Christian is admonish them. This is the same word that was used in **verse 12**. The leaders of the church are supposed to admonish us—which means they are to hold the word of God up before our eyes and say, "This is the standard of the Christian life. This is what we're to do; this is what we're not to do." That is what needs to happen to the idle person—to the person who is out of line. They need to be called to live in accordance with the word of God.

Note that Paul is saying here that the whole congregation is to be doing this to one another. We are not just to leave it to the pastors or the elders; we, as a congregation, are to be exhorting one another in this way. Don't hear this as an excuse to throw your weight around with your fellow church members; it's not about telling people off for anything you don't like. Rather, it's about helping and encouraging your brothers and sisters. If you think you ought to admonish someone, always take time first to read Scripture and ensure that what you are doing is calling that person to live in line with God's word.

Second, "encourage the fainthearted." "The fainthearted" may refer to some of the people who, as we saw in chapter 4 and the start of chapter 5, were struggling because of their concerns about loved ones who had died. These are perhaps people who are very easily discouraged, and they may be those whom Paul means by "fainthearted" here; alternatively, he may be referring to people who are constitutionally timid—or perhaps both. But notice that this time, the other Thessalonians Christians are not to admonish but to encourage. For the fainthearted, the response is not to get on their case but to gently encourage them and strengthen them.

Third, "help the weak." Paul could simply mean the physically weak here; or he could be referring to people who are spiritually immature. Perhaps it could be those people who are stumbling and struggling with sexual immorality, whose sin Paul addressed in 4:3-8. We are not to kick such sinners out but to seek to help them.

So Paul is outlining three different responses for three different kinds of church members. The weak are to be aided; the fainthearted are to be strengthened; those that are out of step are to be confronted and called away from sin—and all members of a church are to do these things to each another. In other words, we are to look out for one another; we are to be concerned about one another's spiritual wellbeing. It's not that we are to become busybodies nor a collective **Big Brother**, spying on one another's lives; it is that we should care enough to engage with one another about important things in the Christian life.

5:4 finishes with an overall instruction. "Be patient with them all."

I so often excuse myself by saying, "I'm just impatient." It feels like being a little impatient doesn't matter as much as other faults. But being impatient is actually being unloving—since 1 Corinthians 13:4 says that love is patient. Patience is an expression of love, and so when I am impatient, I'm actually showing a deficit of love. Impatience is not something to dismiss or excuse; patience is something we should aspire to and be serious about growing in.

> Patience is an expression of love; it is something we should be serious about growing in.

When we see someone who has walked out of line, we are not to snap our fingers at them or snap out our words to them. Rather, we are called to be patient. We admonish them, and we persist in looking out for them. When we see someone who is fainthearted and easily discouraged, we do not become frustrated at their apparent failure to take hold of the promises they have in Christ. Rather, we are called to be patient. We encourage them and remind them that God is their strength. When we see someone who is weak—someone who is stumbling or helpless—we do not ignore them or put a time limit on our help to them. Rather, we are called to be patient. We do all that we can to help them. Patience is to overarch all of our dealings with one another.

Forgiveness and Kindness

In 1 Thessalonians **5:15**, Paul moves on to tell the Thessalonian Christians, and us, how to cultivate a community of forbearance, forgiveness, and kindness.

First, we must "see that no one repays anyone evil for evil." Our standard operating procedure is not to try to get even (or dream of getting even!); it is forbearance and forgiveness. Obeying this command means that our Christian communities will be characterized by forgiveness. Real forgiveness hurts; it is costly. It involves giving up our right to be angry and leaving justice in God's hands. We are capable of really, really messing up with one another, and Paul is telling us not to get even but to forbear. Jesus commanded his people to turn the other cheek (Matthew 5:39), and to do so even when everything in us wants to hit back.

The Lord went on to say that we are not just to forbear but actively to love our enemies and pray for those who persecute us (Matthew 5:44); likewise, Paul says, "Always seek to do good to one another" (1 Thessalonians **5:15**). He is talking about cultivating kindness towards one another: always having in your mind the question "How can I do good to this fellow congregation member, this fellow family member?" This is to live as Jesus did. He refused to revile when he was reviled; he came not to be served but to serve. In other words, our churches should be so gospel-shaped that we will act the way Jesus acted in his earthly ministry to us.

But notice that Paul adds three last words: "and to everyone." This is not just about doing good to one another within the church. Our standard posture toward the world should be to bless and to do good.

This is very important for us to bear in mind as **evangelical** Christians become a smaller and less respected—even increasingly hated—minority in Western societies. Our temptation will be to get mad at secular culture, so that all people will see is our red-faced anger at them and at what they have done to what used to be in many ways a Christian culture. But instead, we should be saying, "We want to do good to you. We want to be good to you. It doesn't matter whether you like us. It doesn't matter whether you hate us. We still want to do good to you." Jesus did good to us when we didn't deserve it and when we were rebelling against him; he died for us, and he spared us by the shedding of his own blood. Our desire should be to reflect that same kind of goodness and kindness and love to the culture around us.

This is the attitude and outlook that is produced by the gospel shaping a local church. May God grant all of us the aspiration to be this kind of church and church member—and then may he by his Holy Spirit work that growth in us.

Questions for reflection

1. "It's not that we are to become busybodies nor a collective Big Brother, spying on one another's lives; it is that we should care enough to engage with one another about important things in the Christian life." How do you reflect on this? What's the difference, practically, between being a busybody and caring enough to engage?

2. When do you find it hardest to be patient? How could you grow in this characteristic?

3. Who do you find it hardest to do good to? What is one thing you could do to show love to someone outside of the church this week?

10. DOS AND DON'TS

Christianity is not a list of rules. It cannot simply be reduced to a series of dos and don'ts. It is a message not about what we do to make ourselves right with God but about what he has done for us—to forgive us, accept us, save us, and welcome us into his family. However, it is not true that there are no commands at all in the Christian life. In 1 Thessalonians **5:16-22**, Paul gives us a list of eight dos and don'ts.

We are not saved *by* our "doing and don'ting"; but we are saved *into* a life of holiness. God saves us so that we can be what he made us to be and do what he made us to do. So these dos and don'ts should never be oppressive commands hanging over our heads to condemn us. They serve as guides, or as standards, for living the life that God has called us to in Christ Jesus.

We all need nudges to do the things that we know we need to do. If you have an exercise regime, you might well need a friend to call or text you in the morning to say, "We're running," or "We're lifting weights," or "I'm going to meet you at the gym." If you have to get to work at a particular time, you might well need a regular alarm to wake you up! It is the same in our spiritual lives: we need reminders.

This is especially true when circumstances are hard. That was the case for the Thessalonians; Paul has already described in this letter the fact that this congregation is under pressure and even under persecution (1:6). How do you live the Christian life when your circumstances themselves could discourage your faith—robbing you of joy, causing you to doubt so much that you have a hard time praying, and derailing you from pursuing holiness by grace? That's when you really need the nudging and encouragement that Paul gives to the Thessalonians in these verses.

These nudges are in three clusters. First, Paul is urging the Thessalonian Christians to pray (**5:16-18**); second, the subject turns to being sensitive to what the Spirit is doing in them (**v 19-21a**); third, **verses 21b-22** can be taken to refer to the actual goal of the Spirit's work in us, which is sanctification.

If we are going to live the Christian life in hard circumstances, we need to have a reason to rejoice even when our circumstances don't supply one. We need a confidence and a thankfulness in prayer that is not derived from circumstances, so that when things are difficult, we call out to the Lord, "Help us! Lord, do something! I'm in a mess! I'm scared! I don't know what to do!" We need a sensitivity to the work of the Spirit so that, when our circumstances could very well drown it out—when a situation is so painful, so disappointing, so discouraging, and so overwhelming that we really can't hear anything else—we still realize that the Spirit is working in us and are able to rejoice in that. And we need to understand what God's purpose is in us and for us and be able to embrace that. Prayer, the Spirit, and God's purpose: these are three things that enable us to live the Christian life when times are hard.

Three Kinds of Prayer

Paul's three instructions in **verses 16-18** all pertain to prayer: rejoice, pray, and give thanks.

Rejoicing could be taken as an overarching attitude which Paul is encouraging; but it can also be expressed in prayer. That's what praise is. Paul is telling us to praise God "always." Second, the instruction to "pray" means specifically intercession—asking God for help. We are to pray for one another "without ceasing." Third, "give thanks" especially refers to thanksgiving in prayer—after all, God is the one we are giving thanks to, the Giver of all good gifts (James 1:17). In all three commands, Paul is urging the Thessalonians—and us—to pray.

We are not only to pray but to keep on praying—"in all circumstances" (1 Thessalonians **5:18**). Paul is acknowledging that there are times and circumstances in which it is difficult to give thanks, to re-joice, and to pray for one another. That is why he's giving these exhor-tations, these nudges. He is saying, *I know you are going through hard times, but I want to remind you that you can still rejoice and pray, even when things seem at their darkest.*

So, we are to rejoice perpetually, to pray continually, and to give thanks invariably. This does not come naturally. What motivation does Paul provide for all this? Think back through the whole letter. One reason to rejoice and pray is the return of the Lord. All the exhorta-tions in this letter are given in light of the Lord's return. Specifically, the content of the end of chapter 4 and the beginning of chap-ter 5, which lead up to this passage, has all been about the return of the Lord. That is one thing that will motivate and encourage the Thessalonians—and you and me—to re-joice always, and to pray without ceasing, and to give thanks in everything. Paul gives the same motivation in Philippians 4:4-5:

> The Lord is always at hand, and that is a reason to rejoice.

"Rejoice in the Lord always; again I will say, rejoice … The Lord is at hand." We rejoice because the Lord is at hand. It is not that things are good—for the Thessalonians, things were bad—but the Lord is always at hand, and that is a reason to rejoice. When we face trouble, it can feel that it is lasting an eternity and that we are all alone in it—but the reality is that the Lord is at hand. The trial is not going to be the last word. He is coming; therefore rejoice.

Another reason to rejoice and give thanks is the fact that God is in charge of everything. "For those who love God all things to work together for good, for those who are called according to his purpose" (Romans 8:28). He is in charge of everything, and he is making everything work for good. There are lots of things in our lives that are not in themselves good, but God is still making them work together *for* good.

Paul also gives us an explicit reason to rejoice and pray within 1 Thessalonians **5:18** itself: "This is the will of God in Christ Jesus for you."

That phrase is not only attached to the exhortation "Give thanks in all circumstances" that we find at the beginning of **verse 18**; it actually goes with **verses 16-17** too. Rejoicing always, praying without ceasing, and giving thanks in all circumstances are all God's will for us.

Here, then, is the ultimate motive for prayer and thanksgiving. He told us to do it! It is the Lord's will. People often ask what the Lord's will is for their life. *Who am I supposed to marry? What job am I supposed to do? Where am I supposed to live?* I don't know the answer to those questions. But I do know that it's the Lord's will for you that you rejoice always, that you pray without ceasing, and that you give thanks in everything. The Lord of the universe has come right out and told us plainly what his will is for our life. That is surely sufficient motivation!

Be Discerning

In **verse 19**, Paul tells us not to "quench the Spirit." He goes on: "Do not despise prophecies, but test everything" (**v 20-21a**).

Paul is clearly speaking of extraordinary prophetic activity. There were genuine New Testament prophets, who could proclaim the revelation of God, but alongside them there were also false prophets, who peddled lies (2 Peter 2:1; 1 John 4:1). Paul has already hinted at some of the misguided beliefs about the second coming of Jesus that existed among the Thessalonians. So this is certainly a call to discernment. Just because somebody stands up and says that their words are a prophecy from God doesn't necessarily believe that it's true! "Test everything," Paul tells us. The Thessalonians should be like the Bereans, who, when Paul taught them the word of God, went and examined the Scriptures to make sure that what he was saying was right (Acts 17:10-12). When people claim they are giving revelatory, prophetic messages, their hearers (and we) should always be going back to the Scriptures to test what such people are saying and see whether it matches up to what God has already revealed in his **inerrant** word.

Equally, Paul seems to be warning the Thessalonians against rejecting out of hand all of this kind of prophetic activity simply because of the way it had been abused. People were claiming to have heard from God who had not done so; but that did not mean that Paul and the other apostles had not received true revelation from God. "Do not despise prophecies" (1 Thessalonians **5:20**), Paul tells us.

Commentators disagree on what exactly he means by "prophecies" and whether or not God speaks afresh in our day. But even when we are not talking about what's called "extraordinary revelation"— specific instances of God speaking—these verses still apply to us. "Do not quench the Spirit" (**v 19**). However we understand the Spirit to be at work exactly, we can agree that he is always after the same thing, whether he is speaking extraordinarily or, as we might say, ordinarily, through his **means of grace**: he is building God's church, equipping us to live in line with God's will, and reminding us of our salvation in Christ and our adoption as God's children. That's the work we must not quench.

"Quench the Spirit" just means "resist the Spirit's work." The Holy Spirit is described as appearing like a fire on the day of Pentecost (Acts 2:1-12). If the Spirit is like a fire, then, in a sense, we are being told not to extinguish that fire.

Perhaps the most obvious way we could do that is to ignore our conviction of sin. The Spirit is always at work to produce conviction of sin in us—godly sorrow that leads to repentance. When the Spirit is convicting us of sin, we must not resist that voice. If he is holding up the mirror of his word and we see our reflection and it does not look good, it hurts. But we must not ignore that. It is a sweet pain, designed to lead us to repentance and grace and forgiveness and joy.

Another way to quench the Spirit would be to delay our response to his overtures. We are on the Holy Spirit's timetable; he is not on ours. The Spirit comes when he wills, to convict us of our sin so that we will repent and change, or to call us to do something for the Lord. We cannot say, "I'll get back to you tomorrow on that."

Acts 24 provides a great example of quenching the Spirit. There, Luke recounts how Paul preached to Felix, a Roman official, and Felix became scared. He stopped Paul during the middle of his sermon, and he said, "Go away for the present. When I get an opportunity I will summon you" (Acts 24:25). Then he left Paul in prison for two years. Those are some of the most frightening words in all of the New Testament. Felix had *Paul* in his presence—Paul, who wrote half of the New Testament! Paul could have opened to Felix the gateway of grace and glory and salvation, but Felix chose to say, *Some other time*, and that other time never came.

A number of years ago, a prominent businessman came to one of our elders and asked him to teach him about time management. So they set up a meeting. When it came to the appointed time, the businessman got there late. Then his smartphone went off perhaps four times in the first three minutes of their meeting—and he answered it every time. The elder closed the book he had got ready and said, "We'll do this some other time, when you're on time and can pay attention." The businessman told me afterwards, "It was a valuable lesson."

That is so often how we are with the Holy Spirit. We need to be respectful and pay attention to him. We need to attend to the means of grace because we never know what and where and when and how it is that the Holy Spirit is going to speak precisely the message that we need to hear. Do not delay your response to the Holy Spirit. You are on his schedule, not your own; and you never know whether there's going to be a tomorrow or not.

A third way to quench the Spirit is simply to think and behave in a way that is contrary to God's will. The Spirit inspired every syllable of the Bible, so we are quenching the Holy Spirit when we engage in behaviors that are contrary to what he says in his word.

I have lost count of the number of professing Christians who have said to me, "I know that the Lord doesn't want me to be unhappy, and therefore I am going to _____." Again and again, the thing they would fill in the blank with is something that the word of God explicitly says that they are not to do. The Holy Spirit has said, *Don't do that.* Yet people still go ahead and do those things. That is to quench the Spirit.

The Spirit Works Good in Us

Paul has two more instructions in 1 Thessalonians **5:21b-22**: "Hold fast what is good. Abstain from every form of evil." How can we do that? Paul tells us the answer in verse 23, as we'll see: because of the work of God the Spirit in us. It is God who sanctifies us. So we love the things that Jesus loves; we hate the things that Jesus hates. We believe the things that Jesus teaches; we reject the things that Jesus rejects. We hold fast to what is good; we abstain from every form of evil. That is the goal of the Spirit's work in us.

This is how to live the Christian life, including in hard times. We remember that the Lord is returning and that it is his will for us to rejoice always, pray without ceasing, and give thanks in everything. We remain sensitive to the Holy Spirit. And we know what he is at work in us to do: to convict and to bring repentance, forgiveness, restoration, and blessing—to make us like Jesus. That is something to base our joy on.

Questions for reflection

1. Do you find it difficult to pray in hard times? How does it help to remember that "the Lord is at hand" (Philippians 4:5)? How does it help to remember that "this is the will of God" (1 Thessalonians 5:18)?

2. Is there any way in which you might be quenching the work of the Spirit in your life at the moment? What will you pray for yourself as a result of reading this?

3. Where can you see the Spirit's work in your life already?

PART TWO

The last thing that Paul said in **verse 22** was "Abstain from every form of evil." That is a comprehensive, demanding **imperative**. *Don't ever sin!* The response to that, from a tender-hearted, conscientious Christian, must be to feel discouraged because we know that even though we love the Lord Jesus Christ and believe the word of God, we *don't* abstain from every form of evil; we do continue to sin. For someone who is serious about fighting sin and growing in grace, a command like "Abstain from all evil" might drive them to despair.

Paul knows that, of course, and he does want to encourage the Thessalonians. He has just told them that he wants them to engage actively in living the Christian life. He wants them to respond affirmatively to the commands that he has given; but he does not want them to be discouraged. So, in **verses 23-24** Paul gives them some sweet encouragement. He writes a blessing—a prayer—for the Thessalonians.

The Work of God

The first reason why the Thessalonian Christians need not be discouraged in the face of the command to "abstain from all evil" is that their sanctification—their growth in holiness—is the work of God in them. It is "the God of peace himself" who sanctifies (**v 23**). Paul doesn't say, *May God aid you as you sanctify yourself*, or, *Lord, would you help them as they try their best to make themselves holy*. He says, "May the God of peace himself sanctify you completely." Of course, there are things that the Christian must do. We have just seen a whole series of commands which believers need to take seriously. But we must understand that God is far more engaged in our sanctification than we could ever be. Even if you are an earnest, serious, Bible-believing, Bible-studying, prayerful Christian, who wants to grow in grace, God is still more committed to and far more active in achieving your sanctification than you are.

After all, he "created [us] in Christ Jesus for good works" (Ephesians 2:10). God's will is our sanctification (1 Thessalonians 4:3). He chose us with a view to making us holy (Ephesians 1:4). He will not tire, he will not falter, and he will not fail in his pursuit of changing us into Christ-likeness. And if God is so committed to this in our lives, we ought to be as well.

The second encouragement in 1 Thessalonians **5:23** lies in how Paul describes God— "the God of peace himself." The God who is at work in us is the God of total well-being and blessing. Peace is a very rich Old Testament concept, meaning more than just not being at war with anyone. The Hebrew word is *shalom*—it means total well-being, complete satisfaction.

Satan continually tells us that holiness is a drag on our happiness— that if we want to be happy, we need to throw holiness overboard. But in fact, happiness and holiness are inextricably connected, because both happiness and holiness come from God. The holy God is also the God of shalom. God wants our total well-being, and none of us can have that apart from sanctification. If we want to be happy, we should seek God. It is in him that we find our ultimate satisfaction.

Complete Perfection

Next, Paul emphasizes the completeness of the task that God is at work in us to perform: "May [he] sanctify you completely, and may your whole spirit and soul and body be kept blameless" (**v 23-24**).

Some theologians have taken these phrases and built on them a doctrine called "entire sanctification." This was part of a movement in the 19th century called Christian Perfectionism, which taught that Christians can attain in this life a state in which they no longer sin. But the truth is that we will never be completely perfect in this life. What Paul is telling us is that we will be made perfect *in the end*—on the last day. His prayer is that the Thessalonians may be blameless "at the coming of our Lord Jesus Christ." That is the day when God will take away all of our sin for good. But he will begin that process now. Paul is not only thinking about what God is going to do in the end but also about what God does throughout our lives. He clearly wants the Thessalonians to make progress in holiness now, though they will never achieve perfection until then. That is why he is praying this prayer.

The way Paul phrases his prayer helps us to have confidence that it will be answered—that all believers really will be made perfect on the day of the Lord's return. Notice the word "kept" in **verse 23**. It is God's purpose to keep us until the end—to hold us and never to allow us to be snatched from the palm of his hand (John 10:28).

John Piper put it very well in a sermon I heard once on Jude v 24-25 (which expresses the same idea): "The fact that I wake up in the morning and am still a Christian is entirely due to the preserving grace of God. God has preserved me." We should never fail to be thankful that the Lord upholds us and preserves us. It is he, and he alone, who can keep us from stumbling— and keep us to the end.

> If I did not know that the sin in me will be eradicated, I could not go on.

"He who calls you is faithful; he will surely do it" (1 Thessalonians **5:24**). That is Paul's culminating thought in regard to our sanctification. The ultimate encouragement for the Thessalonians is not that Paul has prayed this prayer but that the God who has heard it is faithful. That is why we can be confident of his work in us. His promises are yes and amen in Christ (2 Corinthians 1:20), and he will do what he has promised.

If I did not know that the sin in me is going to be eradicated, I could not go on. I'm so thankful for the forgiveness of my sins, but if I thought that I was going to have to eternally deal with my own profound disappointment in myself, and have to keep on being forgiven again and again forever, I couldn't stand it. But thankfully, you and I can have confidence that Paul's prayer will be answered: that by the grace of the God of peace, at the coming of the Lord Jesus Christ, we will be made blameless. God is faithful and has promised to keep his people in his hand. And that is what keeps us going in pursuing holiness now.

The whole of the Christian life hangs upon God's grace, God's promise, God's power, God's faithfulness. When we feel that we are losing in the fight against sin, we can be encouraged: God is working in our life right now. We can live with boldness and assurance because he is faithful.

A Parting Request

It is hard to know how to end a letter. We tend to put in throwaway language that is just picked up from social custom: "Yours sincerely" or "Yours faithfully" or "Best wishes." But as Paul comes to the very end of this letter, his words are filled with significance for the Christian life.

First of all, in 1 Thessalonians **5:25**, he gives a parting request. It is a humble plea for prayer: "Brothers, pray for us."

This is one of three times in these four verses when Paul uses the word "brothers" (which should be understood to include women as well as men). He is drawing attention to the fact that Christians are a part of a family. Christ is our elder brother, and we are part of God's household.

We are being reminded that Paul sees the Thessalonians as his brothers, and he wants them to see him as their brother. This means praying for one another. We have already seen Paul pray for the Thessalonians three times (1:2; 3:12-13; **5:23**). Now he asks them to pray for him. There is humility in that request. Paul had been invested with apostolic authority, he had seen Jesus Christ face to face on the road to Damascus, he had been given Christ's authority over all the churches, he had the capacity to do miracles, he could speak in **tongues**, and he gave real prophecies—and he says to these very ordinary, unremarkable Christians, *Would you please pray for me?*

Paul believed in the power and efficacy of prayer. He knew that God exercises his **sovereign providence** over the world and over the church through the means of the prayers of his people. And he knew that he needed prayer because of the work that he was in.

If you are involved in a gospel-centered church, it is probable that the leaders of your church are praying for you—monthly, weekly, or even daily. Do you pray for them, too? Your ministers stand in special need of prayer. They face satanic opposition because of their ministry. As a pastor and seminary chancellor, I can testify to the need for prayer of those in church leadership. There have been many times where I have felt that the difference between standing and falling was prayer—the only thing between me and collapse was the prayer of God's people. Pray for your ministers.

Final Greetings

In the last few verses, Paul makes his final greetings to the Thessalonians. First he says, "Greet all the brothers with a holy kiss" (**v 26**). In that culture, the holy kiss was an expression of love and fellowship. Different cultures have different physical expressions of fellowship and affection. There are some cultures today where, when you greet people, you always kiss them on the cheek. In some subcultures, there's a lot of hugging. If we do not come from a culture where a kiss is a regular greeting, we do not need to start kissing each other in order to obey Paul's teaching here! The important thing is simply to convey our affection in the way we greet one another. That is how we obey Paul here—we are to show the love and fellowship of the gospel by culturally appropriate physical signs. The gospel creates a family, and those bonds are to be expressed in the life of the local congregation: we are genuinely glad to see one another.

It's easy to experience that and express that in smaller circles in the church. Perhaps you've been meeting with a group of friends for many, many years—people with whom you've prayed and shared triumphs and disaster, joy and heartbreak—and it's easy for all of you to hug one another or shake hands or cry in one another's presence. You naturally break into big, beaming smiles when you see one another. But outside of those circles, perhaps you're not so deliberate in expressing your delight in being a member of the local congregation. All of us ought to be deliberately committed to cultivating a strong, loving fellowship in our congregation and expressing it, not just verbally, but with other culturally appropriate physical expressions. That is what Paul is encouraging this congregation to do.

In **verse 27**, Paul gives a powerful charge. The ESV catches his language very potently: "I put you under oath before the Lord." This is the kind of language we would hear in a courtroom. What is he about to say? Here is what he is charging them to do: "to have this letter read to all the brothers."

This would be a strange thing for you or me to say. If I wrote to someone and put them on oath before the Lord to read my letter publicly before the church, people would be asking why on earth I thought my words were so important. But Paul did have the authority to say this, because he was an apostle: he was invested with special authority by the Lord Jesus Christ (Acts 9:15; Romans 1:1; Galatians 1:15-16). He made this point back in 1 Thessalonians 2:13: "When you received the word of God, which you heard from us, you accepted it not as the word of men but as what it really is, the word of God." Paul is keenly aware that he is not speaking merely human words. Under the inspiration of the Holy Spirit, the letter that he is sending to the Thessalonians is a letter from God.

Paul's strong courtroom language demonstrates to us the importance of listening to the word of God. Do we recognize our need to sit under the word? The reading of the word of God in a public setting is as important as ever. Paul tells Timothy, "Devote yourself to the public reading of Scripture" (1 Timothy 4:13). He tells the Thessalonians under oath to listen to the divinely inspired word. Every congregation needs the word of God to be read to them.

Last of all, Paul gives a parting blessing: "The grace of our Lord

Jesus Christ be with you" (1 Thessalonians **5:28**). Notice that Paul also began this letter with grace: "Grace to you and peace" (1:1). Why? Because grace is the blessing that we all need every day. Grace is not just something that we need at the beginning of the Christian life so that we are forgiven for sins; it is something that we need in order to live the Christian life all the way through.

At the end of his letter, just as at the outset, Paul wants the Thessalonians to rehearse to themselves all that is meant by that wonderful word "grace"—to remember God's free gift to them in Jesus Christ. He had lived for them a life that they could not live and had died for them a death that he did not deserve, so that they might receive a forgiveness for which they did not pay and an eternal fellowship with him that they did not deserve—all at his own expense, freely given. The same is all true of us as believers 2,000 years later. Throughout this letter, Paul has been saying that our growth in the Lord, our maturity in the faith and our sanctification in holiness are dependent upon God being at work in us—which is also an act of grace.

That is why Paul's last word in this first letter to the Thessalonians is grace—grace that is to you, and for you, and with you.

Questions for reflection

1. In what particular areas of your life do you see a need for sanctification at the moment?

2. How do you respond to the idea that it's God's job to keep, hold, preserve, and sanctify us?

3. What do you most want to thank God for after reading 1 Thessalonians?

11. GRATITUDE AND AFFLICTION

The opening greeting of Paul's second letter to the Thessalonian church is strikingly similar to that of his first (1 Thessalonians 1:1—see pages 11-13; the Greek is slightly different but it means the same thing). Here, therefore, we will focus on the two differences.

Our Father

First, Paul twice asks us in 2 Thessalonians **1:1-2** to behold *our* God. This is just a little bit different from 1 Thessalonians; there, he wrote, "in God *the* Father" (my emphasis). Here, he twice says, "in God *our* Father." Paul is pointing to a very important truth about God. He is "our"—*your*—Father. The phrase in 1 Thessalonians 1:1, "God *the* Father and the Lord Jesus Christ," particularly draws attention to the unique relationship that Jesus has with the Father. The Father is the Father of the Lord Jesus Christ, and Jesus Christ is his Son, and, as such, this phrase especially draws our attention to a truth about the triune God. But when Paul says here, "God *our* Father," he's doing what Jesus did when he was teaching his disciples to pray. The prayer Jesus gave them began with "Our Father in heaven" (Matthew 6:9). And the apostle Paul is now saying, *Thessalonians, ponder who your God is. Behold your God; he is your Father.*

Some of us have had good fathers—men of character who loved their wives and children, worked hard, provided for their family, and so on. Others didn't have a great experience of fatherhood and have been left with a void in their heart because of an absence of something that they yearned for. But whatever our experience of fatherhood on earth, every Christian has a heavenly Father, who is quite matchless.

If you had an earthly father who was good, he is but a pale reflection of the heavenly Father. And if you had an earthly father who failed you, then you have a heavenly Father who is not like that at all; in every way that you have been failed, he will never fail you.

The second difference in these opening two verses is that Paul adds, "from God our Father and the Lord Jesus Christ" after writing, "Grace to you and peace" (2 Thessalonians **1:2**—compare 1 Thessalonians 1:1). Where do we get the strength that we need to endure **trials** and to live the Christian life? "From God our Father and the Lord Jesus Christ." Everything that we need to live this Christian life is amply supplied to us. God our Father and the Lord Jesus Christ supply everything that we need—grace (complete pardon) and peace (total well-being).

An Obligation of Gratitude

The very first order of business that Paul has with the Thessalonians is (just as in his first letter) thanksgiving. There are problems in this church, there are trials that they are facing, and there are issues for him to address, but Paul is under a joyful compulsion to thank God for what he is doing in the lives of the Thessalonians. That's what he does straight away in 2 Thessalonians **1:3**.

It's very striking that Paul is under a sense of obligation to give thanks: "We ought always to give thanks to God." And then, just in case we missed it, he adds, "as is right." Those are strong words— "ought" and then "right." Paul is saying that it's not just that he's delighted to give thanks, or that he wants to give thanks, but that he *ought* to give thanks. It's a moral requirement for him.

This is very important. It is a key for fighting discontentment in the Christian life. Discontentment flows, very often, from not having what we want to have. There grows in our minds a connection between what we want to have and what we believe we ought to have. A sense of entitlement grows, and we begin to direct our discontent toward God: "God hasn't given me something that I really deserve to have." Or we can have a growing discontentment because we *do* have something that we don't want to have: something in our life—in our family, in our health, in our circumstances—that is not part of the way we planned it when we started out in life. And we begin to think, "You know what, I really deserve not to have that in my life."

How do we fight that? With gratitude—with thanksgiving. The apostle Paul had more reasons to complain than any of us, and yet he put a priority on thanksgiving. He shows us the way to fight discontentment: by acknowledging the Lord. We need to learn to say, "Lord, whatever good things you've brought into my life, I did not deserve them. They are your gift, and therefore I'm under an obligation to be thankful to you." In other words, we fight discontentment by learning to sense, like Paul, that there is so much to be thankful to God for that we are under an obligation to be thankful to him. In salvation, God has given all of us what we don't deserve; and in not punishing us for our sin, he has not given any of us what we do deserve. That's just the start! When you think about the real, concrete, tangible blessings that God has given you, it will cultivate an attitude of thanksgiving; you will live under a sense of obligation to be grateful. This is not a grudging obligation: "Oh, I have to be grateful." It is a willing obligation: "It would be wrong for me not to be grateful given what God has done for me."

What to Be Grateful For

What is it that Paul is thankful for? "Your faith is growing abundantly, and the love of every one of you for one another is increasing" (**v 3**). He is thankful for the evidence of Christian graces in these believers. And not just the evidence of Christian graces but the fact that the Thessalonians are actually growing; they are maturing in those Christian graces.

In particular, he thanks God that they are growing in faith and increasing in love. Back in 1 Thessalonians 3:12, Paul had prayed that they would increase in love; and in 5:8 he urged them to put on the breastplate of faith and love. Now, here, he is able to give thanks that God has answered his prayers.

This is very important. What are we thankful for? We may be thankful for health and life or job and family, or when we look at our children, we may be thankful for their academic or their athletic or their social success—but are we really concerned about the evidences of grace in their souls, and ours? If you are a parent, imagine God gave you an offer: your child will be godly—filled with faith and growing in love—but they won't be a great student or a good athlete, they won't be particularly popular or physically attractive or end up being financially successful. What would you say to the Lord? What's your priority? What do you really care about?

> Our priorities will show in what we are most thankful for.

Our priorities will show in what we are most thankful for. What Paul is thankful for is actually guiding us to the right priorities. He looks at this congregation and he says, *Lord, they're growing in trust in you! They're trusting your promises, they're believing your gospel, and they're trusting the Lord Jesus Christ in the midst of all their trials and afflictions! They have faith—praise God! Thank you, Lord, that that's happening!*

Paul also sees how they're loving one another. He uses a wonderful phrase to describe their love: "the love of every one of you for one another." This whole congregation is manifesting love to one another. All of them are involved in loving everybody else. This church does not have people who are overlooked and forgotten and on the edges—and it makes Paul's heart sing with thanksgiving. Once again, this is a helpful pointer to what we ought to be thankful for and what we ought to prioritize in the lives of those we love.

Notice that Paul does not thank the Thessalonians themselves for any of this. No: "We ought always to give thanks to *God* for you"

(2 Thessalonians **1:3**, my emphasis). The direction of the thanks is to God. Paul knows that growing in faith and love is the result of God's work in a person. We didn't build our faith; he did. He's the author and finisher of our faith (Hebrews 12:2, KJV). If you're a loving person, you didn't create that love in yourself—God's love created that love in you. Our faith and our love have their origin in the work of the Holy Spirit. The credit goes to him. When we realize this, it humbles us, and it makes us grateful.

Grateful for Perseverance

Next, Paul writes of his gratitude over the result of this growing faith and love in the Thessalonian church: steadfastness in "all your persecutions and in the afflictions that you are enduring" (2 Thessalonians **1:4**). Their growing faith and their increasing love have enabled them to persevere in persecutions and to endure affliction.

The older I become, the more important perseverance and endurance is to me. If you become a Christian as a child and live to be a Christian of 80, you've got to have persevered for more than 850 months! And the apostle Paul is in the business of building Christians who can persevere for a lifetime. They keep on going; they don't quit; they don't stop believing; they don't stop loving; they don't stop growing; they don't fall away; they don't reject the Lord. Paul wants Christians who are in it for the long haul. And so he is led to give thanks that this church, as it faces persecution, is standing firm—it is, in fact, still growing in its faith in Christ and its loving like Christ.

Around the world right now, Christians are being arrested, put on trial, beaten, and worse, all because they hold to the same testimony that you and I do. And most of them, along the way, will be told by their captors or judges, "If you deny Christ, we will release you and drop the charges. There will be no more legal repercussions. You will not face the death penalty." And our brothers and sisters are refusing to do that. They have a steadfastness in persecution. Paul knew some people in the Thessalonian church like that.

We ourselves must be ready for this: ready to refuse to deny our faith because, even in the West, there is more and more pressure on us to deny our Lord, to deny his word, and to deny what we believe. How do we resist that pressure? With increasing faith and love, and with thankfulness. Are you grateful or are you entitled? Are you thankful or are you complaining? And what are you thankful for: for the things that will last forever or the things that will be gone in a matter of years? We need to learn to be grateful for what Paul was grateful for, as we see the evidences of God's work in our lives and in the lives of those around us.

Gratitude for God's grace is what builds the kind of faith and love that leads to us remaining steadfast through the seasons of trial and the times of persecution that, sooner or later, we must walk through. Let grace be both the source of your gratitude and the subject of it.

Questions for reflection

1. How does it help you to remember that, in Christ, God is your Father?

2. What are you most thankful for, and what does that show about your priorities? How can you grow in Paul's kind of thankfulness?

3. What will you pray for your loved ones as a result of reading this chapter?

PART TWO

Next comes a passage about persecution: about enduring trials in light of Jesus' return. Persecution for our belief in Jesus may be an alien thing to us if we live in the West, but it is a constant reality for many of our brothers and sisters in Christ around the world. There are thousands upon thousands of Christians today who know the reality of which Paul speaks in this passage. Even if we do not know that reality personally, we need to be prepared to remain faithful and testify to the truth of the gospel should we be called to bear great cost for our faith.

Afflictions and Persecutions

About the year AD 156, right in the middle of the 2nd century, an 86-year-old pastor from Smyrna in Asia Minor (modern-day Turkey) was arrested by the local Roman provincial ruler for refusing to worship the emperor. His name was Polycarp. He had been appointed to be a pastor in the little city of Smyrna by John the apostle. He was probably about 25 years old when John died. And when the local Roman ruler told him that unless he denied Jesus and worshiped the spirit of the emperor he would be burned at the stake, he refused to recant his love of and trust in the Lord Jesus Christ. This is part of what he prayed before he was burned at the stake: "I give thee thanks that thou hast counted me worthy ... that I should have a part in the number of thy martyrs" (*The Martyrdom of Polycarp*, chapter 14, from Alexander Roberts and James Donaldson, *Ante-Nicene Christian Library*, vol. 1).

It's such a striking prayer. Is that how we would respond if we heard of a Christian who had been killed for their faith? "Lord, thank you that this brother, this sister, has been counted worthy to be numbered among the martyrs"? Is that how we would think about it if we ourselves were called upon to suffer, to be afflicted, or even to die—because of our love and trust in Jesus Christ?

In the early years of Christianity, there was a widespread recognition that it was a very significant blessing and gift from the Lord to be counted worthy to suffer for him. And Paul is talking about that to the Thessalonians here.

Speaking of their suffering, he says it "is evidence of the righteous judgment of God, that you may be considered worthy of the kingdom of God" (2 Thessalonians **1:5**). That's a strange statement to make: persecutions and trials seem to contradict the righteous judgment of God, not to confirm it. If God is sovereign and good, why would his people be suffering and afflicted simply for believing in him? Paul's answer here is that God's righteous judgment is demonstrated—not disproved—by what they are going through. How?

The key lies one verse earlier, back in **verse 4**: Paul boasts of "your steadfastness and faith in all your persecutions and in the afflictions that you are enduring." He is saying that God's just judgment is proven in the Thessalonians staying faithful in the persecutions which are encompassing them. There are two reasons.

First, it justifies God's final judgment. When the righteous endure suffering, God's ultimate punishment of sin—of those who have caused the righteous to suffer—is justified. One of the doctrines that people today hate the most is the doctrine of God's final judgment. Why? Because they say it's unjust; it's unfair. "God ought to forgive everybody," the argument goes: "God ought to accept everybody. So it's mean and wrong to talk about God judging the world." But the truth is that in the face of unjust affliction, there is a moral demand that those causing that affliction be punished. Sin cannot triumph in a moral universe; God punishes the unjust.

When a trial finishes and the verdict is delivered, most of the time people walk out of the courtroom and one party says, "The judge got it right," and the other party says, "The judge got it completely wrong." But in **verse 6**, Paul is pointing out that on Judgment Day, willingly or not, grudgingly or not, everyone will have to admit that the Judge got it right. It is right for God to condemn and punish

injustice and the doers of injustice in this world. That's why the afflictions that the Thessalonians are enduring are evidence of the righteous judgment of God. Paul says it in **verse 6**: "God considers it
just to repay with affliction those who afflict you."

Second, the apostle Paul is saying that as the Thessalonians endure
suffering with faith, God is using even that suffering to sanctify them.
He works through affliction to make people worthy of his kingdom—
so that on the Day of Judgment, it will clearly be just that they are
considered worthy of the kingdom of God. The apostle Peter says
something similar, encouraging us to rejoice because of the way suffering is changing us:

"In this [your knowledge that you have an eternal home,
prepared for you by God] you rejoice, though now for a little
while, if necessary, you have been grieved by various trials, so
that the tested genuineness of your faith—more precious than
gold that perishes though it is tested by fire—may be found to
result in praise and glory and honor at the revelation of Jesus
Christ." (1 Peter 1:6-7)

Persevering in trials is a sign that our faith is genuine. Suffering for
the gospel tests the reality of our faith, and so, as a Christian walks
through that trial with their faith intact, they know a great joy: "Yes,
my faith is real! Yes, God is guarding my faith so that I will reach
my inheritance. Now I know that this faith of mine is genuine, and
always was."

One Future Day

Note that persecuting the Thessalonian church is not the only—and
not the worst—crime committed by these wrongdoers. Not only are
they those who have afflicted the innocent, but they are also those
who "do not know God and ... do not obey the gospel of our Lord
Jesus" (2 Thessalonians **1:8**). So whereas Paul commends the Thessalonians for believing his testimony (**v 10**), these afflicters have not
believed his testimony. As he puts it in his letter to the Romans,

although these people know deep down that they ought to worship God, they have chosen to ignore him and worship something else (Romans 1:21, 25). And these persecutors are in fact doubly without excuse because, although they have heard the command and promise of the gospel—"Believe in the Lord Jesus Christ, and you will be saved" (Acts 16:31)—they have disobeyed that command and turned their backs on that promise. Consequently they will be justly judged. Right now counts forever and refusing to know God and to believe the gospel carries with it eternal consequences.

What is going to happen one future day? "The Lord Jesus is [going to be] revealed from heaven with his mighty angels in flaming fire [and will inflict] vengeance on those who do not know God and on those who do not obey the gospel of our Lord Jesus. They will suffer the punishment of eternal destruction, away from the presence of the Lord and from the glory of his might" (2 Thessalonians **1:7-9**). If you reject Jesus, you will spend eternity apart from Jesus—and that is a serious thing. Paul is deadly serious about the just judgment that awaits all who do not know God. Our response to the gospel will determine eternity for each of us.

Polycarp knew that. When the Roman official who had had him arrested questioned him and demanded that he renounce Jesus and worship the spirit of the emperor, he said to Polycarp, "I will cause thee to be consumed by fire, seeing thou despisest the wild beasts, if thou wilt not repent." Polycarp responded, "Thou threatenest me with fire which burneth for an hour, and after a little is extinguished, but art ignorant of the fire of the coming judgment and of eternal punishment, reserved for the ungodly" (*The Martyrdom of Polycarp*, chapter 11).

Paul has assured the Thessalonian Christians that the injustices they are suffering will be punished. But he doesn't stop there. "God considers it just to repay with affliction those who afflict you, *and to grant relief to you who are afflicted*" (**v 6-7**, my italics). This relief is not only an end to suffering but the joy of seeing the Lord Jesus revealed: "He comes on that day to be glorified in his saints, and to be marveled at among all who have believed" (**v 10**). The Thessalonian Christians—and modern-day Christians too—can rejoice that one day they will see Jesus glorified and join with him in that glory. That's what we're looking forward to. That's what makes the suffering worth it.

Counted Worthy

The fact is that throughout the first generation of Christianity, suffering for the gospel was seen as a matter for rejoicing, a great privilege, and a way in which God refines his people. That should not surprise us since Jesus himself had promised his followers that everyone who loved him would suffer for it (Matthew 5:11-12; John 15:20-21).

In Acts 5, we see the apostles Peter and John imprisoned, beaten up, and threatened. Here is their reaction: "They left the presence of the council, rejoicing that they were counted worthy to suffer dishonor for the name" (Acts 5:41). This view of suffering for the gospel was one shared by ordinary Christians: as Paul put it to the Philippian church, "For it has been granted to you that for the sake of Christ you should not only believe in him but also suffer for his sake" (Philippians 1:29). They viewed suffering for Christ as a gift, just as they viewed faith as a gift from God.

> The earliest Christians would have been worried if they had *not* suffered.

We get worried that we might suffer for Jesus' sake. The earliest Christians would have been worried if they had not suffered. Why are we different in our attitude? I think it's because we don't treasure the Lord Jesus enough. He doesn't mean the world to us. He meant the world to Paul, to the apostles, and to this Thessalonian church. It was a privilege to suffer for him, who had suffered for them, because he meant more to them than anything else in this world.

No wonder Polycarp praised God for giving him a place among the martyrs. It was a gift to him. Polycarp was not saying, *I'm made acceptable to God because I'm getting to die for him.* He was saying, *The Lord has blessed me with the privilege of suffering and dying for his name. He has not only counted me worthy of a relationship with him that I don't deserve; he has counted me worthy of the privilege of suffering for him in this way, which I don't deserve either.*

May it be our prayer that, by God's grace, we should be counted worthy to suffer for his name.

The Mark of True Dependence

In the final verses of this chapter, Paul tells the Thessalonians what he has been praying for them. It's a guide for us as to how we can pray. And it is also a passage which helps us to understand how we go about growing in the Christian life.

The apostle Paul was a man full of **evangelistic** fervor. He was a man with a prodigious work ethic. And he depended upon prayer (2 Thessalonians **1:11**). Why? Because he understood that the mission that he was undertaking was fundamentally a spiritual mission and that he did not have the power to accomplish that mission alone. As hard as he worked to share the gospel and build up churches, he was dependent upon prayer.

I wonder if our prayerlessness in the church today, both individually and corporately, is not only due to the busyness of our lives but to the fact that we do not really understand that the work of God in the hearts of people is a supernatural work. No human being can accomplish it. We have to depend upon God.

Paul is praying for this church "that God may make [them] worthy of his calling." We've already met that phrase in **verse 5**. Paul is praying that God himself, on that great day when these believers stand before the judgment seat of Christ, will declare them worthy of his calling of them. If this depended on Paul, or on the Thessalonians themselves, they would be in trouble. But it depends on God—which is why Paul prays.

This ought to be what we pray for one another. Sometimes a Christian friend will ask us to pray for them about a health or family or vocational circumstance. When we pray for them, we should pray that they would conduct themselves in such a way, in that circumstance, that when they stand before the judgment seat of Christ they would be counted worthy of his calling, by God's grace.

Resolve Is Not Enough

Next, Paul says that he prays that, by God's power, every resolve of these Christians would bear fruit (**v 11**). The truth is, half of growing in grace is wanting to: but only half. God must, by his power, bring good from our resolve. Even when we are committing ourselves to do what is good, we need God's power to actually do it.

This resolve to do good in God's sight is not an attempt to get on God's good side. It is a "work of faith"; in other words, our good conduct is to flow from faith in what Jesus has already done for us and in what he has promised to do.

And it flows from the hope that in the end, "the name of our Lord Jesus may be glorified in you" (**v 12**). John Calvin says about this verse, "He calls us back to the chief end of our whole lives—that we may promote the Lord's glory." Everything we do in the Christian life is to the end that Jesus is glorified. Jesus may be glorified in our situation changing, or he may be glorified in our situation changing not one iota but us persevering in faith. Either should be a cause of joy to us.

The Christian life is not rocket science, but it is impossible without God. You need more than resolve (though you do need that); you need God. You are utterly dependent upon God, his power, and his grace. Your highest aim is to glorify his Son in how you live, whether the times are easier or the times are harder, so that you can hear his "Well done" as you stand at his judgment seat. If we understood that, it would dramatically change the way we go on trying to live the Christian life—and how we view suffering for Christ in our life, and even in our death.

Questions for reflection

1. What kind of suffering might you face—however slight—because of your faith in Christ? When is it especially tempting to try to avoid that suffering and turn away from Jesus?

2. How does the doctrine of God's final judgment help us when we are suffering injustices?

3. What will you pray for yourself in light of Paul's prayer in verses 11-12?

12. DON'T BE DECEIVED

The first part of 2 Thessalonians 2 is one of those passages that commentators mark as one of the most difficult, if not *the* most difficult, to interpret in the entire New Testament. This is, first, because of what Paul says in **verse 3**. He speaks of a "man of lawlessness" or a "man of sin," and no small amount of ink has been spilt over the last 2,000 years by commentators attempting to explain and identify who Paul is speaking of. Second, in verse 7 Paul speaks of "one who now restrains it"—and commentators have probably spent even more ink on what this means than they have on the question that stems from **verse 3**!

This passage has its challenges. But we believe that all Scripture is given by **inspiration** and is profitable for reproof, correction, and training in righteousness (2 Timothy 3:15-16)—which means that even the hard, obscure passages are there to **edify** believers. In this passage, God has something very important to tell us.

Five Anchors

So first of all, what is this passage about? It is "concerning the coming of our Lord Jesus Christ and our being gathered together to him" (2 Thessalonians **2:1**). Once again, we can surmise, questions are being thrown at Paul about the second coming, and in response Paul writes this passage.

A way to approach this passage, to keep it from being intimidating or becoming overly opaque, is to look at some anchor points that Paul gives in the text, so that we remember the big picture of Paul's intentions as he writes this passage. These anchors mean we don't lose track of where Paul is going by heading off on tangents.

1. Paul doesn't want his readers "to be ... shaken in mind or alarmed" (**v 2**). He says it right at the start to show that this is one of the main items on his agenda; he doesn't want the believers to be shaken up and upset in their thinking.

2. Paul doesn't want them to be deceived (**v 3**).

3. Paul wants them to remember what they've already been taught (**v 5**).

4. Paul wants them to remember that in all of this, God is sovereign (That's a summary of verses 7-12.)

5. Paul wants them to know how Satan tries to delude people (v 9-10).

If we keep these five things in mind, the passage will make sense, even if there are aspects of it that remain confusing.

Cultural Expectations

As we have seen, throughout 1 and 2 Thessalonians Paul gives special attention to the coming of Jesus Christ and to how to live in light of that future event. But clearly, this subject was confusing to the Thessalonians, and they were struggling with it. They had evidently had questions for Paul when he was there teaching them. He had had to write them a first letter to clear up some questions and some confusion that they had; and here, in the second letter, he's having to write them again because they're still confused.

Remember, these Thessalonians were predominately, if not exclusively, Gentiles, and they would therefore already have in their minds certain presuppositions about how the end time was going to play out—things that they would have believed since they were little children. If you had grown up in 1st-century Greece, you likely wouldn't have been exposed to the teachings of the Old Testament, and your cultural expectations about the afterlife were therefore going to be very different from what the Bible says (see my comments about 1 Thessalonians 4:13-18 on pages 104-105). You would most likely have believed that, at death, people would enter into a shadowy spiritual world that has no material substance to it. Therefore, when the apostle Paul came to start teaching you about a bodily second coming of Jesus, you would have been left scratching your head. Paul's teaching—that Jesus had been bodily raised from the dead and would return in a physical form, and that believers too would not just be raised in their spirit but in body, so that their whole persons would exist eternally in fellowship with God—simply wouldn't have fit with the cultural water you had been swimming in.

That's the context in which the Thessalonians appear to be asking Paul continual questions about how the end times will play out.

Do Not Be Shaken

Returning to the first anchor point: in 2 Thessalonians **2:2**, Paul says that he does not want them to be "shaken in mind or alarmed." Some of them, we're told here, are afraid that the second coming has already happened. They are scared that the day of the Lord has come and they've missed it! And Paul doesn't want their faith to be unsettled by these things. He is pastorally concerned for them.

The reason why the Thessalonian Christians are troubled is apparently not just that they've had a hard time understanding Paul in the first place but that they've been given some bad information "either by a spirit or a spoken word, or a letter seeming to be from us." Perhaps someone had claimed to have a "word of knowledge"—an alleged prophecy from the Holy Spirit—but one that contradicted or confused them about what Paul had already taught. Perhaps somebody had written them a letter claiming to be Paul and telling them something that, again, was contradictory to what Paul had previously taught. Whichever, they've been unsettled not because of the questions arising from their own minds but because they've gotten hold of some bad teaching. It would be very unsettling to think that the day of the Lord had already come and they'd missed it! Paul doesn't want to leave them in that state.

What Paul says here about not wanting the Thessalonians to be unsettled or alarmed is relevant to all biblical truth. This passage teaches us that it is not a bad thing to wrestle with questions or voice your doubts. Just because we believe in the infallibility, inerrancy, and final authority of Scripture, it does not mean we should be afraid of people struggling with questions. We must be brothers and sisters who ask, and wrestle with, hard questions together, rather than leaving our fellow believers on their own with their doubts.

> We're not afraid of hard questions, but we also don't want to leave people in those questions.

Equally, it is a bad thing to only question things and never reach for, or accept, answers. We're not afraid of hard questions, but we also don't want to leave people in those questions, unsettled in their doubts. We want them to come to understand the truth of God and the truth of his word. That's why Paul is writing: he wants them to be in no doubt of the truth.

That leads us on to the second anchor in **verse 3**: "Let no one deceive you in any way. For that day will not come, unless the rebellion comes first, and the man of lawlessness is revealed." The apostle is saying that there is a definite way in which we can know that we have not missed the day of the Lord. Before the day of the Lord happens, the rebellion will come, and the man of lawlessness will be revealed.

We need to understand *why* Paul is telling them this, before we consider precisely what he is saying. He's saying, *I'm telling you something that means you can know that you've not missed the day of the Lord: the rebellion (or it may be "the apostasy") has not yet*

happened, and the man of lawlessness has not yet been revealed.
The point is, they don't need to worry that they've somehow missed
the day of the Lord.

Who Is the Man of Lawlessness?

That still leaves us with the question: who is the man of lawlessness
(or man of sin, as some manuscripts have it)? For 1,900 years, Christians have worked very hard to identify one of their own contempo-
raries as the leading candidate for this figure. In the first centuries
of the church, before Christianity was a legal religion in the Roman
Empire, the prime candidate was the Roman emperor—perhaps Cal-
igula, who set up a statute of himself in the temple in Jerusalem and
demanded to be worshiped; or Vespasian, whose troops crushed the
temple in Jerusalem and worshiped him there to mock the Jewish
people. After the Emperor Constantine converted to Christianity, the
Roman emperor wasn't such a good candidate for being the man of
sin. Soon, Christians were identifying one or other of the rulers of the
Vandals, invaders from the north who eventually sacked Rome in 455,
as the man of sin.

Then the Vandals were Christianized, and Islam began to spread
through the old Roman world across North Africa all the way up into
Spain, and into eastern Europe through the Balkans almost all the way
to Vienna. Guess who was now named as the man of sin, the man of
lawlessness? Muhammed! Later, in the high Middle Ages, a branch of
Roman Catholic theologians decided that one or other of the corrupt
popes was the man of sin. And then in the 16th- and 17th-century
Reformation, Luther and Calvin and Zwingli and Knox and Cranmer
identified the papacy as the man of lawlessness. The Roman Catholics
returned the favor by announcing that Martin Luther was the man of
sin! It has gone on and on and on.

What do we do with this? We go right back to the word of God
and look at what Paul spells out for us. What are we to be looking
for in the man of sin? We can say three things for sure. First, he is the

"man of lawlessness." He is against the law. He rebels against the law of God and the law of man.

Second, he is a "son of destruction" (**v 3**). It's worth noting that the same phrase was used by the Lord Jesus of Judas Iscariot when he prayed the night before his death. Jesus said to his Father, "While I was with [the disciples], I kept them in your name, which you have given me. I have guarded them, and not one of them has been lost except the son of destruction, that the Scripture might be fulfilled" (John 17:12). This helps us to understand the kind of person Paul is talking about to the Thessalonian church. Judas' sin was to betray Jesus: to actively, consciously work against (as he thought) the glory of the Son of God and the good of his people. This new "son of destruction" will do the same thing.

Though Judas' actions were his own choice, nevertheless they were under God's sovereign hand. Judas sold out his Lord, and that led to the death of Jesus—yet the death of Jesus was, of course, God's plan from before the creation of the world. And so Judas' defeat—his destruction and judgment—was assured. That's what "son of destruction" means, most likely: not just someone who brings destruction but someone who is themselves appointed for destruction. This means that by calling the "man of lawlessness" the "son of destruction" (2 Thessalonians **2:3**), Paul is telling us that however terrifying this man may be, God is still in control. This man is not going to mess up the plan of God because he's already been appointed for destruction by God. He will not win; he will lose.

Third, in **verse 4**, the man of lawlessness "opposes and exalts himself against every so-called god or object of worship, so that he takes his seat in the temple of God, proclaiming himself to be God." In other words, he sets himself up in the place of God.

In verse 11, this is confirmed: "God sends them a strong delusion, so that they may believe what is false." The King James Version reads, "… that they should believe a lie." What's the lie? It's what Paul speaks of in Romans 1:25: worshiping the creature rather than the

Creator. This man of lawlessness is someone created by God, and yet he puts himself in place of God.

One is coming who is going to be against God's law, who will work against God and put himself in place of God; yet he can never defeat God or disrupt God's sovereign plan, and he is destined for destruction. That's what we know about the man of sin. Paul's purpose in saying these things is not to help us to identify exactly who this figure is. It's to warn us: *Don't be deceived. When he comes and he makes his claims, don't you be deceived; make sure you are ready.*

Questions for reflection

1. Is there any teaching that makes you feel "shaken in mind" and "alarmed"—whether it's about the end times or anything else? Who could you talk to about your doubts or confusion?

2. Why is it so important to remember God's sovereignty as we consider what will happen in the future?

3. How anchored are you in biblical truth? What steps could you take to become more certain of what you believe?

PART TWO

The question we are left with by the end of 2 Thessalonians 2:4 is: how do we prepare ourselves to not be deceived by the "man of lawlessness"? Verse 5 gives the answer: we must remember what we have been taught.

God's Word Is Our Defense

The best way to remember what to look out for and what to be on guard against in this spiritual deception—this "mystery of lawlessness," which the man of lawlessness is going to bring (**v 7**)—is simply to go back to the word of God. Paul has not left the Thessalonians unarmed: "Do you not remember that when I was still with you I told you these things?" he asks in **verse 5**.

Back in 1 Thessalonians 2:13, we saw Paul commending the Thessalonians for receiving what he taught them not as the words of men but as what it really was: the word of God. It was doing this that would enable them to discern the difference between truth and deception.

It is no different for us. If we want to avoid being deceived by claims about Jesus that actually stand in opposition to Jesus—claims that would rob him of glory and work against the good of his church—then we must know, remember, and stand on the word of God. This is one reason why we must be in church every Sunday, and read our Bibles on other days too: so that we're not deceived, not taken in by delusion.

God's word will defend us against any kind of false teaching—not just the deceptions of the man of lawlessness when he comes but also any kind of scaremongering about the end times, and indeed any other teaching that contradicts what God has told us in the Bible.

The Scriptures don't tell us every detail about the end times, but they do tell us enough. We've already seen how John 17:12 helps us to understand the "man of lawlessness". There are other places in Scripture that help too. The book of Daniel makes several prophecies which refer to the same figure. In Daniel 8, the prophet Daniel has a complex vision involving a ram, a goat, and a series of horns. Daniel doesn't understand what it means, but the angel Gabriel tells him that it is about "the time of the end" (Daniel 8:17). The ram, the goat, and the horns all represent great kings in history; but in the end will come "a king of bold face" (v 23; see also Daniel 9:26; 11:36-45).

This is a figure of great power—but once again we see that God is greater. Daniel 8 assures us that his power is not his own and it will one day be broken—by a hand that is not human (v 24-25). Daniel 11:45 says, "He shall come to his end, with none to help him."

These visions in Daniel are in some respects difficult to interpret. But the take-home point is the same as that of Paul here in 2 Thessalonians 2: the Lord God is in sovereign control. We don't need to be afraid of the end times. We need to trust in Christ to deliver us safely through them. We need to trust in God's word—not failing to see what it says about the end times and not going beyond what it says.

Who Is the Restrainer?

In 2 Thessalonians **2:7-10**, Paul reminds us again of the simple, reassuring truth that God is sovereign. This is front and center in **verse 7**: "For the mystery of lawlessness is already at work. Only he who now restrains it will do so until he is out of the way."

We may want to respond to Paul's words in **verse 6** by saying, "No, Paul, actually we don't know who the restrainer is"! Commentators disagree over who "he who now restrains it" is. B.B. Warfield, the theologian who was principal of Princeton Theological Seminary from 1886 to 1902, identified the "man of lawlessness" as one (or likely several) Roman emperors, and therefore thought the restrainer was the Jewish state, which stood against Roman godlessness until the destruction of the temple in AD 70:

"The restraining power, on this hypothesis, appears to be the Jewish state. For the continued existence of the Jewish state was both graciously and naturally a protection to Christianity, and hence a restraint on the revelation of the persecuting power. Graciously, it was God's plan to develop Christianity under the protection of Judaism for a short set time."

(Biblical and Theological Studies, p 472)

Most early commentators and commentators today, however, think that Paul more likely had the Roman Empire itself in his mind as the restraining influence on lawlessness. William Hendriksen, one of my favorite commentators, argues that Paul is speaking of the principle of government in general, which restrains evil (see Romans 13:1-5). To arrive at certainty on the restrainer's identity is therefore as unlikely as to say we know for sure who the "man of lawlessness" is. But if we back away from the specific question of who is the instrument of re-straining evil in 2 Thessalonians **2:7**, it's very clear that the main point of **verses 7 to 12** is that it is God who is in control here. Whoever the restrainer of evil is, he or it is simply someone through whom God, the great divine restrainer, operates. He is God's instrument to restrain evil, the principle of lawlessness, and the man of sin. It's God who is in charge here.

This becomes clear when we see what is going to happen when the man of lawlessness is revealed in **verse 8**: "Then the lawless one will be revealed, whom the Lord Jesus will kill with the breath of his mouth and bring to nothing by the appearance of his coming."

> Whoever the restrainer is, it's God who is in charge here.

In fantasy stories, there's almost always a great build-up until the end, when the bad guy and the good guy have a final fight. And in good fantasy stories, the bad guy almost wins, and then the good guy snatches victory from the jaws of defeat. He just about pulls it off, just barely. Well, the contest between the man of lawlessness and the Lord Jesus is go-ing to be nothing like that. This is the biggest anticlimax in history! The man of lawlessness will be revealed, and then Jesus will come and utterly destroy him—not with a sword, not with fire, but with a mere breath of his mouth. This is Godzilla versus Bambi (if Bambi were an evil king rather than a cute, big-eyed deer). Jesus will just destroy him.

In football (American football, if you're reading this outside North America), just like in most sports, there is a great degree of hype. There have been about 35 "Games of the Century" fought in college football in the last 50 years! When the No. 1 ranked team plays the No. 2 ranked team, we're always promised a classic, close game. Sometimes it is. Sometimes, though, one team just crushes the other. It's never close, even from the beginning. And that's what Paul's saying here. When the man of lawlessness is revealed and Jesus comes, it's going to be (in football terms) 120 to nothing. The man of lawlessness is going to have a negative yardage total for the game. Why? Because God is completely in control and Jesus is utterly powerful.

Satan's Playbook

Jesus will win in the end. That is reassuring. But in the meantime, Paul wants us to know what the man of lawlessness will be doing—for he will be influential. He will be powerful, since his work "is by the activity of Satan" (**v 9**). He will deceive those who refuse to believe the gospel and be saved (**v 10**—remember 1:8). And God will confirm people in this delusion, "so that they may believe what is false" (**2:11**).

This lie, as we have said, is that we should worship the creature rather than the Creator. We need here to return to Romans 1, where Paul writes that humans "did not honor [God] as God or give thanks to him ... claiming to be wise, they became fools, and exchanged the glory of the immortal God for images... they exchanged the truth about God for a lie and worshiped and served the creature rather than the Creator" (Romans 1:21-23, 25).

This is the lie. This is the satanic deception that Adam and Eve listened to in the Garden of Eden, and that we all naturally choose to allow ourselves to be deceived by. And God's response to that is to give people over to their choice—in the language of 2 Thessalonians **2:11**, to send them a strong delusion so that they keep believing what they were choosing to believe.

When British biologist and atheist Richard Dawkins wrote his best-selling book that was designed to disprove the existence of God, he called it *The God Delusion*. The apostle Paul, 2,000 years before Richard Dawkins brought up that satanic thought, said to the Thessalonians, *Let me tell you what Satan's big lie is: worshiping the creature rather than the Creator.* It's not Christians who are trapped in delusion; it's those who believe the lie that there is no Creator. And Christians need to know Satan's tactic—to convince us that we should worship a creature, in one way or another.

That doesn't just apply to the end times; it is relevant now. How many of us idolize human talent, beauty, or success? How many of us believe, even without realizing it, that we can solve all our problems on our own if we just go about it in the right way? How many of us prioritize sexual satisfaction over the teaching of God's word, worshiping the body instead of the one who created it? How many of us lay our lives at the altar of wealth, health, and prosperity? We are, all of us, tempted to worship things that are not God; we are tempted every day. And we need to be aware of that temptation.

In most top-level sports, coaches are neurotic about their playbooks being leaked, or their messages to their quarterback or whoever being read by the opposition. In football, in rugby, in tennis doubles, you'll see coaches and players covering their mouths while they're talking so that no one can discover the play that is to come. Not long ago, I saw two football managers on either side of the offensive coordinators holding up towels so that the stadium cameras couldn't pick them up calling the play into their quarterback. They didn't want the defense to know what they were doing ahead of time.

But you and I do know what the devil is doing ahead of time. Paul is reading to us from Satan's playbook. The devil aims to deceive us in every way he can. His last-ditch effort to frustrate the plan of God is going to be to release the man of sin on the world: "The coming of the lawless one is by the activity of Satan" (**v 9**). This is Satan's strategy, and he thinks that he is going to thwart God's plan and frustrate God's rule and worship by the unleashing of this man of lawlessness.

Paul wants to prepare us for the deception of the evil one so that we will stand firm. We live in a world where unbelievers all around are falling for the devil's deceptions—are loving them, promoting them, and are insisting on walking towards condemnation because they "did not believe the truth but had pleasure in unrighteousness" (**v 12**). We must not do the same.

This is a complex passage, and many questions remain unanswered, but the big picture is clear. In his kindness, God has told us the plays that our enemy is going to run before he runs them. Why? So that we can be ready. So that we can remain unshaken by false teaching outside and inside the church, so that we can stand firm in our faith in the Lord Jesus, who is sovereign and who will be victorious, and so that we can look forward to the coming of our Lord Jesus Christ, ready for that glorious moment when we are gathered together to him at last (v 1).

Questions for reflection

1. In what sense is God's word our defense? Do you think this is true in your own life, or do you find you are easily confused by different teachings?

2. In what ways are you most tempted to worship created things in place of the Creator? How could you combat that temptation?

3. Who do you know who is struggling in their faith at the moment or who shows signs of having been deceived by Satan's lies? What could you do to strengthen and encourage them in the truth?

13. TRUTHS TO CLING TO

In the Christian life, there are certain truths that we need to grasp firmly and hang on to in order to persevere as believers in the trials and the tribulations that we must endure. On our way home to glory all of us go "through many dangers, toils, and snares," as John Newton reminds us in the hymn "Amazing Grace." In 2 Thessalonians 2 up to this point, Paul has talked about some of those dangers, toils, and snares—the times of tribulation, the man of lawlessness, and Satan's deceptions. Now he wants to give several truths for us to anchor the Christian life in—to thank God for, to stand firm on, and to hold fast to.

Notice that there is nothing that Paul mentions here as a matter for thanksgiving and as a ground to stand firm on that he has not already taught about in his two letters to this church. For every subject that he mentions in this little section, you will find a precursor to it in 1 Thessalonians or earlier in the letter of 2 Thessalonians. Here, Paul is bringing to their minds truths that he has already taught them, and he's telling them, *I want you to hold fast to these truths.* There are four such truths in **2:13-14**:

1. The love of God (**v 13**)

2. The choice, or the **election**, of God (**v 13**)

3. The sanctifying work of God's Holy Spirit in us (**v 14**)

4. The calling of God (**v 14**)

The Love of God

Notice what Paul calls the Thessalonians in **verse 13**: "brothers beloved by the Lord." He wants them to realize again and reflect upon the fact that God himself, the Father, has set his love on them. From before the foundation of the world, the Father has loved them. Paul wants these believers to relish the reality of the love of God for them.

Do you meditate on the love of God for you? In a sense, it's one of the hardest things to believe. If you know yourself and if you've admitted that you are a sinner, it's not easy to believe that God knows you *and* that God loves you. Yet here is Paul encouraging us to acknowledge and stand firm in the love of God. He wants us to take it in, and to think and live as though it is true—because it is!

It's dangerous to live the Christian life without knowing the love of God for you. Here is the truth about every single Christian: God loves you. It is not that he loves you because you have faith in Christ; no, you have faith in Christ because he loves you. So as believers, we need to work on an experiential understanding of God's love for us; for if we do not, it's going to leave us crippled somewhere in the Christian life. It's a dangerous place to be in, to not know the love of God for you. But it's a wonderful life to live when you know that God really does love you.

The Comfort of the Doctrine of Election

Second, Paul thanks God for his election. The idea that God chooses people is a doctrine that many Christians like to argue about. But Paul never sees election as something merely to be discussed; he sees it as something that is absolutely critical to the comfort of believers. He gives thanks to God for it: "We give thanks to God for you, brothers beloved by the Lord, because God chose you as the firstfruits to be saved" (**v 13**).

There is a translation issue here. Some Bible translations, including the ESV and NIV, render this clause, "God chose you as the firstfruits."

In each, a footnote alerts us to an alternative translation: God "chose you from the beginning." The reason is that one Greek letter separates the two meanings—and some manuscripts have it written one way while others have it written another. Therefore, Bible scholars debate what the best rendering of this passage is. Paul does use the term "firstfruits" at least five other times in his writings, but I think probably the best rendering of this passage is "chose you from the beginning," simply because it fits the context better. It's the idea that Paul speaks of in Ephesians 1:4-5: "[God] chose us in [Christ] before the foundation of the world, that we should be holy and blameless before him. In love he predestined us for adoption to himself as sons through Jesus Christ, according to the purpose of

> Underneath and behind our decision to trust Jesus is God's choosing of us.

his will." I think that's what Paul is getting at here. He's saying, *I thank God that in his love for you he chose you from the beginning, before the world was.*

We are chosen by God. Did we seek the Lord? Yes, we did, but we sought the Lord because he had chosen us. We love him because he first loved us, and we have believed in him because he first chose us. Paul is grounding the **assurance** of the Thessalonians in the fact that God chose them. Jesus did the same with his disciples: "You did not choose me, but I chose you" (John 15:16). Why was that important for his disciples to understand? Because all of them were going to abandon him in his hour of need. Judas who betrayed him, Peter denied him, and all of the disciples deserted Jesus as he was arrested and put on trial and crucified (Matthew 26:56). But he had said to them, "You did not choose me, but I chose you." What determined the security of the disciples was Jesus' choice, not theirs.

Do we make a decision to follow Christ? Yes, we do, and we must. Do we trust in Christ? Yes, we do, and we must. But underneath and behind our own decision to trust Jesus, from before the foundation of the world, is God's choosing of us—and that's the only thing that can keep us comforted and certain and secure. If it depended on us to keep walking by faith through the trials of this life, and through all that Paul has spelled out in 2 Thessalonians 2:1-13, we would have every reason to fear and to panic. But it depends on the unchanging God, and we can find deep assurance in that—especially when we suffer and when we sin.

The Spirit's Work and the Calling of God

Third, Paul speaks of the Thessalonian Christians' sanctification, or growth in godliness: "God chose you ... to be saved, through sanctification by the Spirit and belief in the truth" (**v 13**). Notice how he's emphasizing both God's role and our role in our salvation. Our belief in God's truth, in God's word, is the key instrument that God uses on the human side to grow us in grace. But salvation isn't just about us doing it on our own; it's about what God the Spirit is doing in us. This is why Paul does not thank the Thessalonians for their increasing godliness; he thanks God. And he calls these Christians to remember what the Spirit is doing—to believe that God is at work in them to make them more godly.

There is a sense in which we *have been* saved—we have believed in the truth of Jesus' gospel and have been forgiven of our sin once and for all. But there is also a sense in which our salvation is *ongoing*. This is the sanctification by the Spirit. The Lord Jesus has not simply taken our punishment for sin; he has given us his Spirit to cleanse us of our sinfulness. Not that we will ever be completely perfect this side of the new creation. But we are being refined and prepared for the place of perfect righteousness, where we will one day make our home.

This is what Paul speaks of fourthly and finally, in **verse 14**: the calling of God. What are these Christians called to? To "obtain the glory of our Lord Jesus Christ." The apostle Paul is saying to those Thessalonians, persecuted as they are, in the midst of tribulation as they are, that their future is one in which they will obtain the glory of the Lord Jesus Christ.

That's what we, too, are called to; that is the end point of our salvation. In this life we will have trials, but we are waiting for "an inheritance that is imperishable, undefiled, and unfading" (1 Peter 1:4). Perhaps you feel tarnished by life—dragged down by difficulties and traumas—or that you are simply too ordinary to amount to much. Life may not feel glorious now. But one day we will see Jesus face to face.

And we do have a taste of this glory even now, as we get to know Jesus and become more like him here on earth. On the night before he died, Jesus prayed to his Father, "The glory that you have given me I have given to [those who believe in me], that they may be one even as we are one, I in them and you in me" (John 17:22-23). Do you wonder what Jesus' glory means? Look at believers who cling to Christ even when sufferings come; who are unified in Christ despite seemingly insuperable differences; who speak of Christ as one whom they know. These are glimpses of the glory to which we have been called.

Truths to Cling To

Paul is not telling the Thessalonian church these truths merely so that they can understand them but so that they might cling to them. He wants them to *know* these things so that they "stand firm" on them— for then they will not be "quickly shaken in mind or alarmed" (2 Thessalonians 2:2) by false teaching, by trials, or by their own sinfulness. He wants them to dig their fingers into these truths and hang on.

In **verse 15**, Paul calls on the Thessalonian Christians to "stand firm and hold to the traditions" that he has given to them. He's not talking about extra-biblical tradition. In the New Testament, tradition is good to the extent that it is faithful to God's word, and bad if it is not. When it's merely the traditions of men or human invention, it's always bad. So we find Jesus in Matthew 15:3-9 criticizing the traditions of men, and we find Paul here in 2 Thessalonians **2:15** commending traditions because they are biblical. Remember that Paul is an apostle, commissioned by the risen Jesus to teach the truth. We can treat all his teaching as what it is: the word of God (1 Thessalonians 2:13).

Back in 1987 Henry Dempsey, a commercial pilot, was flying a small commuter plane from Boston, Massachusetts to Lewiston, Maine. He didn't have any passengers on board; he and his copilot were just moving the plane to Lewiston. While they were out over the Atlantic Ocean, they heard a strange noise in the back of the plane, and so Dempsey got up out of the pilot's seat, left the copilot to fly the plane, and went to the back of the plane to try to figure out what the rattling was. As he pushed on the door at the back of the plane, it fell open, and he fell out of the plane—halfway. He grabbed onto the railing of the boarding steps and hung on for his life, 4,000 feet above the Atlantic Ocean and traveling at 200 miles an hour.

His copilot looked back, saw the back door of the plane open, and assumed that Dempsey had been pulled out of the plane. So he called for the coastguard to search the ocean for someone who had fallen out of a plane and made an emergency landing at the nearest airfield. When they landed, Henry Dempsey was still hanging on to the railing of the stairs at the back of the plane, his head twelve inches off of the ground as they landed. When the emergency services reached him, they literally had to peel his hands free from the railing, because he was holding on so tight.

Paul is saying to us that he wants us to wrap our hands around these truths—the truths of the love of God, the election of God, the sanctifying work of God the Spirit in us, and the promise of future glory—and refuse to let go. He wants us to hang on for dear life, just like Henry Dempsey hung on to the railing of those boarding steps to keep from being thrown from that plane. It's absolutely essential for living the Christian life to hold fast to these truths. That way, we will stand firm and know confidence and joy in our Christian lives.

Questions for reflection

1. Do you ever struggle to believe in God's love for you? How would it change your life if you believed more in this truth?

2. What glimpses of Jesus' glory do you see in the Christians around you?

3. Which of the truths highlighted in this chapter do you most need to cling to at the moment?

PART TWO

My Great-Aunt Marjorie would write me and my brothers on most of the significant occasions in our childhood—birthdays, Christmases, school graduations—and then even in later parts of life when significant things came along. In her letters she gave spiritual encouragement and then told us what blessings she was praying to God for us to experience in life. Most of the toys I received in childhood are long forgotten, but those letters I still have, and I treasure them to this day. Some of them actually hang on walls in various offices, and when I look at them, I'm reminded of what my Great-Aunt Marjorie prayed for me. The words in those letters represented for her the deep aspirations of her heart for me and for my brothers, for my mother and my father, and for the many others to whom she wrote. And what she was writing were benedictions.

Paul, too, loved writing benedictions, and we have one here in the last two verses of 2 Thessalonians 2, in just a single sentence. Some scholars of early Christianity call these benedictions "wish prayers" because they have their roots in similar prayers of blessing or expressions of wishes for blessing in someone's life. You would find pious 1st-century Jewish people praying these "wish prayers" for one another.

Today, benedictions are things that many people overlook. In many churches, including those of my own **Presbyterian** denomination, a benediction is pronounced weekly at the end of the service, and it is the point at which many begin to think about their pot roast; it simply signifies that the church service is over and they're about to get to go home. (I'm aware that some start thinking about their pot roast well before the benediction!) Equally, others care deeply about benedictions; I've had people give me ratings on mine!

One striking aspect of Paul's benediction here is that it does not come at the end of his letter. He will end this letter with a benediction (3:18), as he usually does in his letters, and he began with one too (1:2). But here, at the end of chapter 2, he provides for us another beautiful benediction, and it's appropriate because it comes at the end of a chapter that's been filled with many dangers, toils, and snares. This chapter has spoken of the man of lawlessness and some great tribulations that are to come for believers—it is, in many ways, a fearsome chapter. The Thessalonians have been asking questions that have frightened and disturbed them, and Paul has given them answers, but some of the answers themselves must have generated some fear. And so, as these believers think about living life and enduring trials in light of Jesus' return, Paul pronounces a blessing on them. He prays to God to bless them in a specific way, and that's very helpful—for us, as for them. This prayer of blessing represents Paul's deep aspiration—his profound desire for blessing from God to his Thessalonian brothers and sisters. It repays us to pay attention to each part of it, because this whole blessing is a blessing to all who receive it by faith.

The Divinity of Christ

It would be easy to skip over the phrase with which Paul begins in **2:16**. But actually we should revel in it. These words were written less than 20 years after the crucifixion and resurrection of Jesus Christ; so what we read here reflects the settled belief of the very earliest Christians. Paul is about to pronounce a blessing on the Thessalonians from God—but *before* he mentions "God our Father," he says, "Now may our Lord Jesus Christ himself…"

Bear in mind that Paul was once a Pharisee, who grew up in a strain of Judaism that took the Old Testament Scriptures extremely seriously. He believed that there is one God; and he knew that the very first of the Ten Commandments is "You shall have no other gods before me" (Exodus 20:3). On the other side of his conversion on the Damascus road (Acts 9:1-9), he still believed that truth: there's only one God, and we should have no other gods before or beside him. Yet here Paul is pronouncing a benediction in which he says, *"May the Lord Jesus … and God our Father" bless you.*

This is significant because it is a powerful testimony to the full divinity of Jesus Christ. Paul is not just putting Jesus and the Father together in the same sentence, as he often does (for instance, 1 Thessalonians 1:1 and 2 Thessalonians 1:1-2). Here, he puts Jesus first! This is a powerful testimony to the full divinity of Jesus Christ. No godly Pharisee would ever have put someone before God who wasn't God! But Paul understood that there is one God, who has eternally existed in three Persons—the Father, Son, and Holy Spirit—and he believed that the Father was not the Son, and the Son was not the Father, and the Father was not the Spirit, and the Spirit was not the Father, and so on and so on. He believed that the Father, the Son, and the Holy Spirit were distinct, but that they were in the one God. And so he was ready to offer worship to Father, Son, and Holy Spirit, and he would speak of the divinity of each without denying the unity of all.

Here is a powerful testimony to the full divinity of Jesus.

One God. Three Persons. And so in **2:16**, Paul speaks of "the Lord Jesus Christ" before he speaks of "God our Father." Both are Persons in the Trinity, both are fully God, and both are to be worshiped as such.

That is hard to say in a few sentences and impossible to fully understand, given the finite nature of our human minds. (A god whose nature we could fully understand with a human brain would be a fairly limited sort of "god".) It took the Christian church over 400 years to figure out how to speak about these truths. The Nicene Creed, a statement of core Christian belief, was formulated in 325 at the Council of Nicaea, slightly amended in 381 at the Council of Constantinople, and then slightly amended once more and finally affirmed at the Council of Chalcedon in 451. And here is what it says about the Lord Jesus: "We believe in one Lord Jesus Christ, the only-begotten Son of God, begotten of his Father before all worlds, God of God, Light of Light, very God of very God, begotten, not made, being of one substance with the Father."

Each part of that sentence was designed by the members of the Councils of Nicaea, Constantinople, and Chalcedon to affirm emphatically both the deity of Christ and the oneness of God. Note that they came up with the wording, but they didn't make up the doctrine. That doctrine goes all the way back to the earliest days of Christianity, and Paul is articulating it here in **verse 16**. It's a powerful testimony to the deity of Christ. In his commentary *The Message of Thessalonians*, the late British pastor and theologian John Stott says about this little phrase:

> "We notice how once again Paul couples the Father and the Son. He did it in 1 Thessalonians 1:1 and 3:11. But this time he startles us by even putting the Son before the Father. It is amazing enough, within twenty years of the resurrection, that Paul should have bracketed Jesus Christ with God; it is yet more amazing that now he brackets God with Jesus Christ. He also goes on, in spite of the plurality of the subject (Father and Son), to use the singular reflexive *who* and the singular verbs *loved* and *gave*. Paul is evidently quite clear … about the equality and the unity of the Father and the Son." (p 179)

That's exactly right. We should not skip over this little phrase. When we come to worship on the Lord's Day, we come to worship the divine Savior, the Son of the living God, **begotten**, not created. We come to worship him as God. That's not a metaphor for us. Jesus is not simply a great moral teacher. He's not merely a prophet. He is the Son of the living God. That is the essence, the uniqueness, of Christian worship—we worship Jesus as divine, fully God and fully man, in one person.

The Loving and Giving Father

Next, we learn something about our heavenly Father in this benediction: about "God our Father, who loved us and gave us…" (**v 16**). Paul is pointing to two things in particular that he wants us to remember about God: God loves, and God gave.

This letter was almost certainly written before John wrote his Gospel, but it reflects the same theology of the nature of the Father: "God so *loved* the world, that he *gave*..." (John 3:16, my emphasis). John and Paul both taught that our heavenly Father, sovereign as he is, mighty as he is, awesome as he is, is loving and giving.

That God the Father should love us and should give to us is particularly astonishing not only when we consider who he is but who we are. As Thomas Benson Pollock's hymn "We Have Not Loved Thee as We Ought" puts it,

> We have not loved thee as we ought,
> Nor cared that we are loved by thee...

I identify with that. I know that God, in Christ, has loved me, but there are some times when I don't live or act like I care that God loves me. I don't make as big a deal about that as I ought to. I don't experience that like I ought to. I need to pray what Pollock does later in the same stanza:

> Lord, give a pure and loving heart
> To feel and own the love thou art.

Perhaps we need this prayer more and more as we go on in the Christian life. At the beginning of a relationship, it's easier to "feel and own" the love of another person. But as time passes, that love can become familiar and be taken for granted. If you've walked with God for many years, you may well have felt, in the first flush of your conversion, as if you could have reached out and touched Jesus right there. But over time, it is easy to become cold to him. We need to pray, "Lord, help me feel and own the love of God for me." He stands ready to do so—for he remains the God who loves and who gives.

Comfort and Hope through Grace

God loves, and God gives. Paul describes what God has given us as "eternal comfort and good hope through grace" (2 Thessalonians **2:16**).

- ■ *Eternal comfort:* This means more than comforting someone in a bad time; it's the old meaning of that term, denoting strengthening and encouraging (so the NIV translates it "encouragement"). God has given and still gives his children encouragement, strengthening, and comfort. This is the kind of comfort that strengthens us when we are mourning or suffering or being persecuted. And it will never go away.

■ *Good hope:* William Hendriksen writes, "The good hope of which Paul speaks is a hope that is well-founded, namely, upon God's promises, Christ's **redeeming** work, etc., is full of joy, never ends in disappointment, and has its object in God Triune" (*1 & 2 Thessalonians,* p 189).

■ *Through grace:* We have this eternal comfort and good hope not because we deserved it or earned it or worked for it or added our good deeds to our faith to secure it; no, we have it given to us by God through grace.

The Blessing

In one sense, Paul still hasn't even got to the blessing prayer yet. Rather, he's reminding the believers in Thessalonica that they are already blessed. God has already given them eternal comfort—strength that nobody can take away from them; and he's given them good hope—hope that nobody can take away from them. He's given them these things as a free gift, which means that nothing they can do will change his mind. They—and we—already enjoy these things.

Now, in **verse 17**, Paul finally gets to the blessing! He wants the Thessalonians, and us, to be encouraged and to be equipped.

He wants our hearts to be comforted—again, this word means "strengthened" or "encouraged." Paul has just said that God has already given them encouragement, but they, and we, can never get too much.

Then Paul says he is praying for God to "establish [their hearts] in every good work and word." The Christian life isn't just sitting around and contemplating the blessings that the Lord has given us.

The Christian life is living out of the blessings that God has given us. Paul wants us to do and be what God made us to do and be. He wants us to be equipped for every good work and word. He wants every word and every work of ours to glorify God. That's what we were created, and recreated in Christ, to do.

When we realize that, we will probably think, "Lord, I'm going to need some help with that." Precisely! That's why Paul is pronouncing a benediction on us. *Lord, strengthen them, encourage them, comfort them, and then equip them and establish them so that every word and every work glorifies You.* That is a blessing that Paul prayed not just for the Thessalonians but, under the inspiration of the Holy Spirit, for all of us—and we need it. This is a blessing that we would do well to ask "our Lord Jesus Christ ... and God our Father" to grant to us and to those whom we love.

Questions for reflection

1. How easy do you find it to "feel and own" God's love for you? What could help you with this?

2. What "good work and word" do you need God's help with this week?

3. Who could you pray for using the words of Paul's benediction?

14. CONFIDENT PRAYERS

Paul begins 2 Thessalonians 3 with a "Finally," indicating that he has finished the main argument of the book. Yet he still has a chapter to go—he is doing what many preachers do, by saying, "And in conclusion" and then going on for a while! But in Paul's case, he has a particular reason. It's as though he's looked back over the letter that he's written so far (or perhaps dictated to his secretary), and seen that there are some exhortations and encouragements that he wishes to add. So in these verses, we have a two-part prayer request (**v 1-2**); a two-part expression of confidence (**v 3-4**); and a two-part **benediction** (**v 5**). Then, in the remainder of the chapter, Paul continues with some further commands and warnings (v 6-15) and a last benediction to close with (v 16-18).

Praying for Speed

The Greek original for "Brothers, pray for us" (**v 1**) indicates something obscured in our English translations, which is that Paul is asking the Thessalonians to keep on praying rather than to start doing something they have not been doing. He knows they're praying for him and his cowriters, and he'd like them to continue to pray. He asks them to pray specifically for two things.

The first thing is "that the word of the Lord may speed ahead and be honored." Paul's language comes right out of the psalms: "He sends out his command to the earth; his word runs swiftly" (Psalm 147:15). Paul seems to have this psalm in mind as he asks the Thessalonians to pray that the word of the Lord may travel swiftly. It's a prayer for the spread of the gospel and for the success of the gospel. If you ever wonder, "How should I pray for my ministers or for evangelists, church-planters, missionaries, and faithful preachers in other churches?" this would be a great prayer. We should be praying for the spread and the success of the gospel as God blesses the gospel work of his people. Paul is asking the Thessalonians to do this, and we need to do this, because Paul's faithfulness and abilities, and the faithfulness and abilities of to-day's gospel ministers, are not what brings success. God's blessing is what causes the spread and success of the gospel.

Of course, the Thessalonians themselves were evidence of God's blessing in ensuring that his word sped ahead. Back in 1 Thessalonians 2:13, Paul had told them he was praising God because "when you received the word of God, which you heard from us, you accepted it not as the word of men but as what it really is, the word of God, which is at work in you believers." Now he's asking them to be concerned for the ongoing spread and success of the gospel by being diligent in prayer for him in his missionary endeavors.

One of the ways that you know that the gospel has taken hold of your heart is that you care about the gospel taking hold of other people's hearts. If you don't care about the spread of the gospel—if you don't care about other people coming to faith in Christ as the gospel changes their hearts and lives—it's doubtful that your life has ever truly been changed by the gospel; because those who have been transformed by the grace of God—who have grasped the undeserved, Christ-bought forgiveness of God—want everybody to experience that. And so, if the gospel has taken hold of my heart, then I will pray as Paul directs his Thessalonian brothers and sisters to here.

Praying for Deliverance

Paul's second prayer request is in 2 Thessalonians **3:2**: "Pray ... that we may be delivered from wicked and evil men." This is not theoretical for Paul. There were those who dogged his steps everywhere he went in Asia Minor, trying to undermine the teaching and the doctrines that he was proclaiming. There were people who contradicted the glorious gospel of free grace that he was preaching. Presumably, in their own minds Paul's opponents were doing something that was good and right; but Paul calls them "wicked and evil." To oppose the gospel and hinder gospel ministry is a serious thing. So Paul asks the Thessalonians to pray for deliverance from such people.

In our own day, more and more, we will need to pray this prayer. Hindering the gospel is now more possible legally in the US, and throughout the West, than it has ever been. The gospel is closed down when it offends because to cause offense is increasingly considered not as a necessary by-product of the free exchange of ideas but rather as a hate crime. So the gospel itself is closed off, shut down, and forbidden in those settings where it causes offense. We need to pray for church-planters and campus ministers and evangelists and missionaries and ministers because there are people who want to hinder the spread of the gospel. And we need to pray that our churches themselves will be free of those who, while claiming to be Christians, actually prove to be ashamed of the gospel and act against its spread.

Why Paul Is Confident

After asking for these two prayers to be lifted up for him and for his companions, Paul then assures his readers that he is very confident of what God is doing. He speaks of a double confidence—about what the Lord is doing *for* the Thessalonians and about what the Lord is doing *in* the Thessalonians.

In 2 Thessalonians **3:3**, Paul says that he is fully confident that God will strengthen and guard these Christians. The original language here is ambiguous. "He will ... guard you against the evil one" could be translated "He will ... protect you against evil"—that is, evil in general rather than a personal evil force. But Paul is clearly thinking of personal opposition to the Thessalonians. Evil and wicked men were seeking to hinder them in their ministry, so here Paul is thinking of the evil one and how he wants to attack the Thessalonians.

Elsewhere Paul is very clear that there is a supernatural, personal force in this universe that wants to destroy us (see for example what he said about Satan in 2:9), even as he is confident that the Lord will deliver us from that evil one. It is worth asking ourselves: do we ever factor in this reality? In the struggles that we experience in life—whether they be in marriage or family or vocation or some other arena—do we keep in mind (and in prayer) that the evil one is seeking to destroy God's people? I'm not talking about blame-shifting; I'm not talking about finding a demon under every rock; but I am talking about acknowledging the reality of a supernatural, personal force in this universe who wants to destroy us—"a roaring lion, seeking someone to devour" (1 Peter 5:8). Do we realize that it's not just our sin and the opposition of the world that we have to be on the lookout for? The world, the **flesh**, *and the devil* are all arrayed against the Christian. When we realize this, it will change the way we pray against opposition: we will acknowledge that we are in a battle which only the Lord can win. Only if we know this will we truly appreciate what Paul is saying here: that he is confident that the Lord will establish and guard us against the evil one. He is with us; he will not leave us or forsake us. He will protect us. And that is a tremendous truth, which we so often forget right when we need to remember it.

> We are in a battle which only the Lord can win.

I remember, a few years ago, reading a Facebook post from a minister whom I had taught when he was a student at the seminary where I serve. It said this:

"Sixteen times in the Bible God says, 'I am with you.' Twelve times in the Bible he says, 'I will not leave you.' Eight times he says, 'I will not forsake you.' So please, tell me, what's got you so worried?"

It's a really good point. So often we forget God's promises that he is with us, that he will not leave us, and that he will not forsake us. Here in 2 Thessalonians **3:3**, Paul is trying to remind us of that. The Lord will establish and guard us. We must forget neither that there are powerful spiritual forces ranged against us nor that our Lord is greater than all of them.

Paul's second ground of confidence comes in **verse 4**: "We have confidence in the Lord about you, that you are doing and will do the things that we command." In other words, Paul is confident about the Thessalonian church because he sees them obeying what the apostles have taught—they are a living embodiment of Matthew 28:20, seeking to observe all that the disciples were taught by the Lord Jesus. But notice who Paul says his confidence is in: "We have confidence *in the Lord*" (my emphasis). This isn't just Paul's confidence in the Thessalonians; it's his confidence in what the Lord is doing in them.

Most Christians are still struggling with some of the same things that we were struggling with 20 years before. But there may well be some things about which we look back and think, "I used to struggle to understand that, to obey in that way, to fight that temptation, and I don't struggle in that way anymore." That is not down to being a wonderful person! It's the Lord's work in us. The word of God has washed over you and washed over you and washed over you, and the Lord has been at work through that to change you in that area. And Paul sees that happening in the Thessalonians, and it gives him confidence in their ongoing faith and growth.

Strength to Endure

Next, Paul speaks a double blessing to these Christians: "May the Lord direct your hearts to the love of God and to the steadfastness of Christ" (2 Thessalonians **3:5**). First, he wants them to look at, to know, to experience the truth that God loves them. This has been a running theme through these two letters to this church (most explicitly in 2 Thessalonians 2:13, 16). And Paul is praying it for the Thessalonians again.

Second, Paul is asking the Lord to direct them "to the steadfastness of Christ" or "to the endurance of Christ." In other words, Paul is saying that he wants them (and us) to look squarely at the endurance of Jesus Christ for us. Paul is calling us to endure in our trials and tribulations; but God never asks us to endure more than he has endured himself. When it comes to enduring in the Christian life, we can look at Jesus' endurance for us. He endured poverty, suffering, pain, sorrow, rejection, mocking, torture, and death. He endured all of those things for us. So when God calls us to endurance, we should contemplate the endurance of Christ for us.

When I was in my early fifties, I found a notebook that I hadn't seen for over two decades. I opened it up and it was a portion of a journal that I'd kept about 25 years previously. I am a terrible journaler—I tend to journal for about three days in every six months, at best. And then I forget that I ever journaled. But I rediscovered this journal, and as I read my words there, it was clear that I had thought that I was going through the worst thing that could ever happen to me and that the world was about to come to an end. As I looked back on that journal, I imagined a conversation with my 26-year-old self. I told him, "Buddy, you have no idea! What you're going through now is nothing compared to the things that are ahead! You think the world is coming to an end—let me tell you, it's a walk in the park!"

If 26-year-old Ligon had been directed to older Ligon—to the truth that older Ligon had walked through those trials in his twenties and that he would walk through harder times in future years—it would have put things into some perspective for him. But what 26-year-old Ligon truly needed (and what Ligon still needs, decades later) was to be directed to "the endurance of Christ." Contemplating his endurance will encourage us, and it will give us perspective.

Jesus has already endured for us, so that he is able to empathize with us in the very real things that we have to endure even as he beckons us on and assures us we can come through. But not only that—what he endured was far, far greater than anything that we will ever be called upon to endure as believers. And it is on that basis that we can know that we really can endure, with faith and obedience intact. He loves us. He has endured before us and for us. And he is faithful in establishing and guarding us. Therefore, we can joyfully pray for and work for the word of the Lord to speed ahead and be honored, whatever forces are ranged against us.

Questions for reflection

1. How much do you pray for the leaders of your church? How could you pray for them—and for your church in general—along the lines of Paul's prayer requests in verses 1-2?

2. What difference do you think it would make to your life to acknowledge the work of the evil one more? Why is that important?

3. What evidence do you see of the Lord's work in your life? What struggle do you need his continuing help with?

PART TWO

In 1 Thessalonians 5:14, among the exhortations that Paul gave was "admonish the idle." It seems that there were some people in the Thessalonian church who were expecting Jesus to return immediately, and so they quit work and depended upon the benevolence of other (still working) Christians to take care of them. Paul told them to keep working! But apparently the problem had not disappeared. In 2 Thessalonians **3:6-15** that little phrase "admonish the idle" is expanded into a whole section. In fact, Paul spends as much time on this issue in his second letter as he does on the second coming.

Paul uses very strong language here. He does not just warn those who are idle—he tells other believers to keep away from them (v 6)! Three times the word "command" is used (**v 6, 10, 12**). Paul is like a general in an army ordering his officers to do this or that. This shows Paul's apostolic authority; he has the authority to command the church. It also shows what a serious problem idleness is. This is not just a minor failing; it is a major problem in the church (as we'll see). At the same time, Paul also employs gentler pastoral language. He uses the words "brothers" or "brother" three times too (**v 6, 13, 15**). So Paul is underlining both his authority over the church and his relationship with the church as he seeks to bring the word of God to bear on the lives of the Thessalonian Christians.

Paul has a series of specific exhortations in this passage:

1. "If anyone is not willing to work, let him not eat" (**v 10**). The believers are not to become a financial burden to others unnecessarily.

2. "Such persons we command ... to ... work quietly and to earn their own living" (**v 12**). This exhortation is the positive counterpart to the first.

3. "Do not grow weary in doing good" (**v 13**). This is an exhortation not only to the people who are idle but to the whole congregation.

4. The congregation as a whole is not to encourage or enable or associate with those who disobey Paul's teaching on this particular point: "Have nothing to do with [those people] that [they] may be ashamed" (**v 14**).

Of course, it is unlikely that any of us have quit work because we think that Jesus is coming imminently and are now expecting everybody else to feed us! But there are still general applications from this passage for all of us because Paul is working from general principles of the Christian life to apply them to this specific situation. And of course those general principles still apply to us.

So here are the three general principles upon which Paul bases his specific teaching about idleness prompted by a wrong response to the reality of Christ's return.

An Expectation of Obedience

Paul expects the word of God to be obeyed in the church. This is why Paul uses the words "command" and "obey" repeatedly in this passage. There are many well-meaning Christians today who think that if we believe in grace, there's no room left for obedience and duty in the Christian life. Clearly, the apostle Paul did not think that. He both preached grace and emphasized obedience. The key is to understand where obedience fits in the Christian life. Christians do not believe that we obey to get God to love us. We do not obey in order to save ourselves but because we have taken Jesus as our Lord and King. We are his disciples. We are his subjects. We want to be like him. The apostle Paul expects the word of God to be obeyed in this congregation, and in yours and mine.

As a motivation for obedience, Paul first emphasizes his own teaching and then his own example. First, the behavior of those who are living idly is "not in accord with the tradition that you received from us" (**v 6**). In other words, Paul has already told the Thessalonians that Christians are not to be lazy. Christians know that humanity fulfils our **creation mandate** partly through work (Genesis 1:28; 2:15); and so it is a glorious thing, even though it is, in this fallen world, also a toil-some thing. It is in line with Scripture to work hard.

Second, Paul points out his own practice. He was not idle (2 Thessalonians **3:7**). Despite the pressures and demands of his gospel work, he and his companions did not "eat anyone's bread without paying for it, but with toil and labor we worked night and day."

In 1 Timothy 5:17-18 and in 1 Corinthians 9:3-7 and 14, Paul makes it clear that the normal pattern is for congregations to support their pastor. But in this case, Paul supported himself and did not ask for money from the people that he was ministering to. He did not want to burden them unnecessarily.

We need to embrace this work ethic in our own day and time—not making more of work than we should nor sliding into idleness, but working hard to glorify our God and ensure that we do not unnecessarily burden others. "Whatever you do, work at it heartily, as for the Lord and not for men" (Colossians 3:23).

Do Not Grow Weary

Paul's second principle is this: not to grow weary in doing good (2 Thessalonians **3:13**). It seems that the majority of the congregation has become discouraged by this minority that has stopped working. We can imagine them throwing up their hands in frustration; they've had enough! And Paul is turning to them and saying, in effect, *I know that what you're dealing with is frustrating. I've had to write to you twice about this. It's frustrating to me too! But don't stop doing the right thing.*

We can so easily grow weary of doing the right thing when there are people around us—in our own congregation even—who are not living in accord with the Bible. That is so discouraging. It makes for cynical or bitter or proud believers. It sows the thought, "Why bother?" But Paul does not want us to listen to that voice. He wants us not to be distracted by others' wrongdoing but to continue to pursue holiness.

Do Not Condone

Paul then says, "If anyone does not obey what we say in this letter, take note of that person, and have nothing to do with him, that he may be ashamed" (**v 14**). He is telling the obedient Christians not to condone, approve, or enable those who are not doing good and who will not listen to the command to repent and start obeying. In other words, he is calling for the church to discipline those who are disobeying.

When we think about discipline in the church, very often we think it is the job of the minister or the elders. But here, Paul is speaking to the whole con-gregation. He's saying that if there are people who are refusing to stop sinning even when they have been called out on it from God's word, other Christians must not condone that or tacitly approve of it. They must not even associate with them. Every church member needs to play an active part in the mutual accountability of their local church.

> Every church member needs to play an active part in mutual accountability.

What is the point of this discipline? "That he may be ashamed." This is a way that some people are brought to repentance because it shows them that this is not accepted. This is not just an alternative way of living as a Christian; this is wrong, and it is serious.

I've seen it happen in churches I have served. I've seen men go and confront other men in their congregation and say, "Brother, you are not living like a Christian." I've seen women say lovingly but firmly to their sisters in Christ, "You're not living like a Christian." And I've seen those courageous words, said humbly and with tears, bring people back from acting in a way that is out of accord with God's word.

That difficult work is what Paul calls the obedient Thessalonian Christians to here, as they struggle to deal with those who insist on living idly. He tells them to keep doing good. But he also tells them to make clear in their actions towards the idle that their actions are disobedient and serious.

Finally, Paul reminds them that these are family members, not enemies (**v 15**). These are people who are acting out of accord with God's word, but Paul still wants to win them back. Despite his firmness and frustration, he is still being pastoral. There's a desire for reconciliation—a desire for reclamation. May our churches be like the church Paul was calling the believers in Thessalonica to be. May we, as individuals, be swift to repent when we need to, slow to give up on doing good, and clear with our brothers and sisters when they falter and wander. May we always be willing to seek and celebrate repentance and reconciliation.

Reason for Hope, Hope for Peace

In **verse 16** Paul turns to his final benediction—asking "the Lord of peace himself [to] give you peace at all times and in every way." He is saying that only the Lord of peace can give us real peace—and he is able to give it to us at all times, in all ways, in all places, and in all circumstances.

This congregation was facing trials of every kind. From the outside, they were facing pressure and persecution—and that persecution would increase. But there were also troubles *within* this congregation—from those who were misunderstanding, perhaps wilfully, Paul's teaching about Christ's return, and causing concern and division. This church needed a sense of peace.

For Paul, unity mattered; it was (and is) one of the signs that the gospel is true. Paul loved the fact that Jews and Gentiles (who, in that day and age, had very little to do with one another and very little good to say about one another) had come together in local churches in shared love for and worship of their Messiah. Division was a big deal for Paul—and it should be for us—because it undermined gospel witness. So the Thessalonians needed peace not only within themselves but also between themselves. They needed unity, and that can only come from the Lord of peace—the one who died on the cross for all his people. We cannot look down on brothers and sisters when we are on our knees together before the throne of grace.

The Presence of Christ

Next Paul prays, "The Lord be with you all." These words of Paul echo Jesus' words from the end of the Gospel of Matthew: "I am with you always" (Matthew 28:20).

The 20th-century author Frederick Buechner, in speaking about the blessings the Lord gives and the trials the Lord calls his people to go through, said:

"The grace of God means something like: 'Here is your life. You might never have been, but you are, because the party wouldn't have been complete without you. Here is the world. Beautiful and terrible things will happen. Don't be afraid. I am with you. Nothing can ever separate us.'" (from *Wishful Thinking*)

What we need in the darkest places of life is to know that we're not alone in them but that the Lord is with us. The peace of the Christian is only possible because of the presence of the Lord—and the peace of the Christian *is* the presence of our Lord.

No Peace without the Grace of God

Paul is not yet done. In 2 Thessalonians **3:17-18**, he writes his final words with his own hand. He takes the stylus from the hand of the **amanuensis**. (Evidently he had been using someone to take down his dictation.) He writes his final words with his own hand so that the Thessalonians will recognize his writing and know that this letter is genuine.

With his own hand, Paul scrawls out the words, "The grace of our Lord Jesus Christ be with you all" (**v 18**). How appropriate. Paul had no doubt pronounced that benediction on them verbally. Now they're reading it in Paul's own handwriting. For the grace of God is the reason why we can enjoy peace with God and his people, and the grace of God is the reason why we can enjoy the presence of God.

One last thing: we must not miss the "alls" of these final verses. There are three (and one "every"!). This is the apostle's doctrine of "no Christian left behind." He knows there are some who are on the edge in this congregation, but he wants them all to know this peace, and to know Christ's presence, and to receive Christ's grace. It is as they all grow together in their experience and enjoyment of the grace, peace, and presence of the Lord Jesus Christ that they will hold fast to the truth and walk with endurance in their trials, until the day the Lord Jesus returns. And that is no less true for our churches today.

So Paul's prayer then is my prayer for you now:

"Now may the Lord of peace himself give you peace at all times in every way. The Lord be with you all. ... The grace of our Lord Jesus Christ be with you all."

Amen.

Questions for reflection

1. When are you tempted toward idleness? What will it look like for you to "work heartily, as for the Lord" (Colossians 3:23)?

2. How do you respond when you see people around you persisting in sin? How does it affect your own faith? How does this passage help you in this kind of situation?

3. In what ways do you or your church need peace at the moment? How does it help to know that Jesus is the gracious Lord of peace?

GLOSSARY

Abraham: the ancestor of the nation of Israel, and the man God made a covenant (a binding agreement) with. God promised to make his family into a great nation, give them a land, and bring blessing to all nations through one of his descendants (see Genesis 12:1-3).

Amanuensis: a literary assistant who takes dictation from an author or copies manuscripts.

Apostasy: the abandonment of religious belief.

Apostle: a man appointed directly by the risen Christ to teach about him with authority.

Ascension: when Jesus left earth to return to heaven, to sit and rule at God the Father's right hand (see Acts 1:6-11; Philippians 2:9-11).

Assurance: a believer's trustful confidence that they have been saved through Jesus Christ and that therefore they are accepted and loved by God.

Baptism: a public church ceremony involving water (either through immersion or sprinkling) by which someone is welcomed into the church as a member of God's people, through faith in Jesus Christ. Bible-believing Christians differ over whether baptism should be given to children of Christians or to those who are professing faith in Christ themselves.

Baptist: a Christian, church or group of churches that baptize those who are professing faith in Christ themselves (rather than the children of Christians), usually by immersion in water (rather than by sprinkling it).

Begotten: brought into existence by a parent, or as if by a parent. This word is traditionally used to capture something of the order of the three Persons of the Trinity. Father, Son, and Spirit are all eternal (i.e. never created). By saying that the Son is "begotten" of the Father, we mean that the Father is the first Person of the Trinity and the Son the second (the Spirit is the third). The Son is equal to the Father in deity, not subordinate to him; but he is different in role.

Benediction: a declaration of "good words" from God. Benedictions are found throughout Scripture and often recited at the end of a church service.

Big Brother: originating from George Orwell's dystopian novel *1984*, this means an authority with complete power seeking to limit and control people's thoughts as well as behavior, especially by comprehensive surveillance.

Commentator: an author of a commentary, a book that explains parts of the Bible verse by verse.

Conversion: the moment when someone for the first time recognizes Jesus, God's Son, as Lord, and turns to him as Savior.

Covenant: a binding agreement or promise. The old covenant set out how believers in the Old Testament related to God; Jesus established the new covenant, so believers now relate to God through Jesus' saving death and resurrection.

Creation mandate: God's words to Adam and Eve (see Genesis 1:28) which form his ongoing command to humanity to be fruitful and multiply (= have children), and to fill and subdue (= cultivate) the earth.

Cynic philosophers: ancient Greek philosophers who aimed to live in agreement with nature, enjoying only the bare necessities of life, and taught that people should free themselves from influences such as wealth, fame, and power.

Deacon: literally, a table-waiter; in the church, deacons are church members appointed to serve the church in practical ways.

Disciples: those who follow Jesus and trust him as their Lord and Savior; the disciples of Jesus most often referred to in the New Testament were twelve men whom he chose to be his closest friends and followers.

Doctrine: the study of what is true about God; or a statement about an aspect of that truth.

Edify: build up fellow believers in the Christian faith.

Election: the teaching that God has chosen to give saving faith to some specific people, so that they become Christians. (These people are the elect.)

End of the age: the future point in time when Jesus returns to this world, God's judgment takes place, and Christ's kingdom takes full effect in the new creation.

Episcopal Church: a denomination of churches governed by bishops.

Ethics: a set of moral principles.

Evangelical: Christians or churches that emphasize the Bible's authority and the need to be personally converted through faith in Jesus' death and resurrection.

Evangelist: a person who tells non-Christians the good news of Jesus Christ and equips other Christians to do that.

Evangelistic: anything (e.g. a book, talk, meeting) that aims to proclaim to non-Christians the good news of Jesus Christ.

Exhortations: speech or writing that aims to strongly persuade, inspire, or encourage people to do something.

Fallen world: our world as it is today, adversely affected in every part by the consequences of Adam and Eve's sin when they disobeyed God by eating the forbidden fruit (see Genesis 3).

Flesh: our natural desire to sin.

Fruit of the Spirit: the characteristics that the Holy Spirit grows in Christians, including love, joy, peace, patience, kindness, goodness, faithfulness, gentleness, and self-control (see Galatians 5:22-23).

Functional: actual, real.

Gentiles: people who are not ethnically Jewish.

Grace: undeserved, overflowing generosity.

Graces: characteristics of a believer that have been given and grown by God.

Hades: the name that the ancient Greeks and Romans gave to the underworld (the place beyond death); also the name of the Greek god of the underworld.

Hebrew: a Jew, a member of Israel.

Holiness: the characteristic of being pure and set apart for God.

Hypostatic union: the union of two natures, one fully human and one fully divine, in the one person Jesus Christ.

Imperative: a command or order.

Inerrant: true and without any fault or error.

Infallibility: the doctrine that the Bible will not lead us astray in matters of faith and practice.

Inspiration (of Scripture): the doctrine that God the Holy Spirit closely influenced those who wrote Scripture such that the words of the Bible are not merely human in origin but also the words of God.

Judea: a Roman province in the south of present-day Israel, once part of the ancient kingdom of Israel, and which included Jerusalem.

King David: the second king of Israel, and the most important king in Old Testament history. He also wrote many of the psalms.

Lamb: a title for Jesus (see John 1:29; 1 Peter 1:18-19; Revelation 5:6-14); it derives from his sacrificial death as the perfect atonement for sin, which had been foreshadowed in the Old Testament by sacrifices to God of animals such as lambs for the forgiveness of sins.

Lord's Day: mentioned by the apostle John (Revelation 1:10), it's generally assumed that this refers to the first day of the week (our Sunday), when the first Christians would gather together.

Means of grace: ordinary ways (as opposed to supernatural ones) through which the Holy Spirit works to build up Christians and enable their perseverance in the Christian faith; they include the gathering of the church, the preaching and reading of God's word, discipleship, prayer, church discipline, baptism, and the Lord's Supper.

Ministry: the work of someone who cares for others. It includes preaching and teaching about Jesus as well as caring for physical needs.

New covenant: see "covenant."

Old covenant: see "covenant."

Ordained: publicly appointed someone to a position of pastoral and teaching leadership in a church.

Pagans: a New Testament word for those who are non-Christians (e.g. 1 Peter 2:12; 4:3-5). Pagan religion (generally speaking) refers to a belief system including many gods who are unpredictable, and whose favor or blessing or protection needs to be bought or earned through ritual or sacrifice.

Parable: a memorable story that illustrates a truth about Jesus and/ or his kingdom.

Pastor: from the Latin for "shepherd," this means a church minister—that is, someone who has been given oversight of a church congregation.

Paul: the author of most of the New Testament letters. Paul was a very religious Jew and originally a leader in persecuting the first Christians; he was dramatically converted to the Christian faith (see Acts 9) and became the last man to be appointed by Jesus Christ to be an apostle. He was given the particular responsibility of teaching the Christian good news to non-Jewish people.

Pentecost: a Jewish feast celebrating God giving his people his law on Mount Sinai (Exodus 19 – 31). On the day of this feast, 50 days after Jesus' resurrection, the Holy Spirit came to the first Christians (Acts 2), so "Pentecost" is how Christians refer to this event.

Peter: originally called Simon and often referred to as Simon Peter, he was one of the Twelve, the closest followers of Jesus, and a leading apostle in the 1st-century church. He was the author of two New Testament letters and probably the eye-witness source of Mark's Gospel.

Pharisee: a member of a Jewish group who lived by strict observance of both God's Old Testament law and Jewish tradition. They mistakenly thought their law-observance made them right with God.

Pit: the realm of the devil and his evil spirits (see Revelation 9:11).

Polytheistic: believing in many gods.

Predestined: chose in advance. God chose in advance to save certain people out of his great and undeserved love, rather than on the basis of their character or actions.

Presbyterian: a denomination of Christian churches governed by elders.

Professions of faith: declarations of becoming a Christian.

Professing: claiming to be something (e.g. a professing Christian is anyone who says they are a Christian).

Puritans: members of a 16th- and 17th-century movement in Great Britain that was committed to the Bible as God's word, to simpler worship services, to greater commitment and devotion to following Christ, and increasingly to resisting the institutional church's hierarchical structures. Many emigrated to what would become the US and were a strong influence on the church in many early colonies.

Redeeming: this word describes how Christ has freed his people from slavery to sin and death by dying on the cross.

Reformation: a 16th- and early 17th-century movement in northern Europe that re-established the gospel of justification by faith and the preaching of God's word as central teaching and practice in many churches, and which opposed the Pope and the Roman church.

Reformer: someone from one of the first two generations of people in the 16th century who preached the rediscovered gospel of justification by faith, and who opposed the Pope and the Roman church.

Ruling elders: (in Presbyterian churches) those elected by the congregation to serve as a voting member of the church's decision-making council (a teaching elder, by contrast, functions as a church minister).

Sabbath: Saturday; the holy day when Jewish people were commanded not to work (see Exodus 20:8-11).

Saints: a biblical term for all Christians.

Sanctify: make holy or make more like Christ, by the work of the Holy Spirit.

Son of Man: a title that Jesus often used of himself; it derives from Daniel 7:13-15, where Daniel sees in a vision that the Son of Man is given by God everlasting dominion, glory and a kingdom, and all nations serve him.

Sovereign providence: the all-powerful care of God, who, with supreme authority and complete control, oversees everything that happens and directs events for the good of his people.

Spiritual weapons: ways of resisting the devil and his attempts to make us give up our faith in Christ. In Ephesians 6:13-17, the apostle Paul pictures reliance on the truths of the gospel as armor that will enable us to stand firm against the devil.

Stephen: the first Christian to be killed for his faith (see Acts 6 – 7).

Superlatives: phrases that convey the best or the worst or the highest degree or greatest extremity of some characteristic or quality.

Synagogue: local place of worship, prayer, and teaching for Jewish people.

Testimonies: true stories of how God brought individuals to faith in Jesus.

Theology: the study of what is true about God, or a particular understanding or interpretation of what is true about God.

Thessalonica: a city in present-day north-eastern Greece. During his second missionary journey, Paul visited the synagogue there for three Sabbaths (Acts 17:1-9), and as a result, some people became Christians, and a church was formed.

The Law and the Prophets: Jewish shorthand for the Old Testament.

The Way: a 1st-century name for the Christian faith (see Acts 9:2; 19:9, 23).

Tongues: literally "languages." Christians differ over whether this word, as used in the New Testament, refers only to human languages or includes non-human, supernaturally-given languages.

Trials: difficult or testing periods of life. For example, a time of ill-health, or persecution, or loneliness, or unemployment.

Trinity: the biblical doctrine that the one God is three Persons, distinct from one another, each fully God, of the same "essence" (or "God-ness"). We usually call these three Persons Father, Son, and Holy Spirit.

Word of knowledge: one of the gifts of the Spirit listed in 1 Corinthians 12: 8-10. The precise nature of this gift is unclear; Christians differ over whether it is an insight supernaturally given by the Spirit or simply an ability to grasp and teach biblical truths.

Worldview: the beliefs we hold in an attempt to make sense of the world as we experience it, and which direct how we live in it. Everyone has a worldview.

Wrath: God's settled, deserved hatred of and anger at sin.

BIBLIOGRAPHY

■ Frederick Buechner, *Wishful Thinking: A Theological ABC* (Harper and Row, 1973).

■ John Calvin, *Commentaries on the Epistle of Paul to the Philippians, Colossians, and Thessalonians*, translated by John Pringle (Calvin Translation Society, 1851)

■ Matt Chandler et al, *Joy in the Sorrow* (The Good Book Company, 2019)

■ Adolf Deissmann, *Light from the Ancient East: The New Testament Illustrated by Recently Discovered Texts of the Graeco-Roman World* (Hodder and Stoughton, 1911)

■ William Hendriksen, *1 & 2 Thessalonians*, in the New Testament Commentary series (The Banner of Truth Trust, 1972)

■ Leon Morris, *1 & 2 Thessalonians*, in the Tyndale New Testament Commentaries series (IVP, 2009)

■ J.I. Packer, "Some Perspectives on Preaching" (*Ashland Theological Journal*, 1990)

■ Alexander Roberts and James Donaldson, *Ante-Nicene Christian Library*, vol. 1 (T & T Clark, 1867)

■ John Stott, *The Message of Thessalonians*, in The Bible Speaks Today series (IVP, 1991; this edition, 2006)

■ B.B. Warfield, *Biblical and Theological Studies* (The Presbyterian and Reformed Publishing Company, 1952)

1 & 2 Thessalonians for...
Bible-study Groups

Ligon Duncan's **Good Book Guide** to 1 & 2 Thessalonians is the companion to this resource, helping groups of Christians to explore, discuss, and apply the messages of these letters together. Eight studies, each including investigation, application, getting personal, prayer, and explore more sections, take you through the letters. Includes a concise Leader's Guide at the back.

Find out more at:
www.thegoodbook.com/goodbookguides
www.thegoodbook.co.uk/goodbookguides

Daily Devotionals

Explore daily devotional helps you open up the Scriptures and will encourage and equip you in your walk with God. Available as a quarterly booklet, *Explore* is also available as an app, where you can download Ligon's notes on 1 & 2 Thessalonians, alongside contributions from trusted Bible teachers including Tim Keller, Sam Allberry, Albert Mohler, and David Helm.

The Whole Series

- **Exodus For You** *Tim Chester*

- **Judges For You** *Timothy Keller*

- **Ruth For You** *Tony Merida*

- **1 Samuel For You** *Tim Chester*

- **2 Samuel For You** *Tim Chester*

- **Nehemiah For You** *Eric Mason*

- **Psalms For You** *Christopher Ash*

- **Proverbs For You** *Kathleen Nielson*

- **Isaiah For You** *Tim Chester*

- **Daniel For You** *David Helm*

- **Micah For You** *Stephen Um*

- **Mark For You** *Jason Meyer*

- **Luke 1-12 For You** *Mike McKinley*

- **Luke 12-24 For You** *Mike McKinley*

- **John 1-12 For You** *Josh Moody*

- **John 13-21 For You** *Josh Moody*

- **Acts 1-12 For You** *Albert Mohler*

- **Acts 13-28 For You** *Albert Mohler*

- **Romans 1–7 For You** *Timothy Keller*

- **Romans 8–16 For You** *Timothy Keller*

- **1 Corinthians For You** *Andrew Wilson*

- **2 Corinthians For You** *Gary Millar*

- **Galatians For You** *Timothy Keller*

- **Ephesians For You** *Richard Coekin*

- **Philippians For You** *Steven Lawson*

- **Colossians & Philemon For You**
  Mark Meynell

- **1 & 2 Thessalonians For You** *Ligon Duncan*

- **1 & 2 Timothy For You** *Phillip Jensen*

- **Titus For You** *Tim Chester*

- **Hebrews For You** *Michael Kruger*

- **James For You** *Sam Allberry*

- **1 Peter For You** *Juan Sanchez*

- **2 Peter & Jude For You** *Miguel Núñez*

- **Revelation For You** *Tim Chester*

Find out more about these resources at:
www.thegoodbook.com/for-you
www.thegoodbook.co.uk/for-you